COVER STORIES

Celebrating Tournament Program Cover Art

FROM THE CROSBY CLAMBAKE &
AT&T PEBBLE BEACH NATIONAL PRO-AM

A Charitable Classic Since 1947

MORE THAN $85 MILLION GENERATED
FOR CHARITY THROUGH 2010

MONTEREY PENINSULA FOUNDATION
BOOK PROJECT STAFF
Ollie Nutt
Steve Worthy
Amanda Evans
Cindy Zoller Silver
Cathy Scherzer
Dianna H. Panes

INSIGHT EDITIONS
Publisher: Raoul Goff
Creative Director: Iain R. Morris
Designers: Barbara Genetin & Dasha Trojanek
Design Assistant: Gabe Ely
Managing Editor: Kevin Toyama
Project Editor: Scott Gummer
Copyeditor: Mikayla Butchart
Production Director: Leslie Cohen

ISBN: 978-0-615308-80-7

Sponsor Edition ISBN: 978-0-615311-37-1
Limited Edition ISBN: 978-0-615311-38-8

PHOTO CREDITS
Pages 1, 2–3: Marc Howard Photography
Pages 68, 90–91, 112–115, 137–139:
Property of the AT&T Pebble Beach National Pro-Am

TITLE CREDIT
Ed Vyeda

Insight Editions
3160 Kerner Blvd., Unit 108
San Rafael, CA 94901
www.insighteditions.com

ROOTS of PEACE   REPLANTED PAPER

Palace Press International, in association with Roots of Peace, will plant
two trees for each tree used in the manufacturing of this book. Roots
of Peace is an internationally renowned humanitarian organization
dedicated to eradicating land mines worldwide and converting war-torn
lands into productive farms and wildlife habitats. Together, we will plant
two million fruit and nut trees in Afghanistan and provide farmers there
with the skills and support necessary for sustainable land use.

Manufactured in China by Palace Press International
www.palacepress.com

10 9 8 7 6 5 4 3 2 1

"*I* *always looked forward to playing in the Crosby. I only remember missing one, in 1970, the year my father passed away in February. The week became a Nicklaus family tradition; one of my greatest joys is playing golf with family and friends, and I was fortunate over the years to share the experience with my sons. I also partnered with President Gerald Ford several times, and from that grew our long-standing friendship. Among the hardest things I ever had to do was to ask the President, after a number of years of playing together, if I could play with my son Jack. I remember he said, 'I wish that I would've been able to do more things with my boys, and I applaud you for that.' That's the kind of gracious, family-oriented man Gerald Ford was.*

The event was good fun—the clambake, the celebrities, the entertainment. But it was good golf, too, and a tough tournament to win. One of the most embarrassing moments of my entire life came one year when we had some friends back to the room after the round to celebrate my birthday (January 21). Everyone was having a good time, and it was kind of loud when the phone rang. My friend John Swanson called to wish me a happy birthday and said he was with someone who wanted to say hello. Because of the noise I could barely hear this guy singing 'Happy Birthday' to me. When he finished I said, all very polite and business-like, 'To whom am I speaking, please?'

'Oh,' said the voice, 'this is Bing Crosby.'

He said he was a little hoarse, but I still cannot believe I did not recognize that voice."

—JACK NICKLAUS

"*A* *ll in all, my career in golf has been exciting and rewarding and I have no real regrets. But I did have a few disappointments along the way. I never won that fourth major, the PGA Championship, or the old Crosby, now the AT&T Pebble Beach National Pro-Am. The tournament has always been one of the prestige events on the Tour. The courses and the scenery, the format and the celebrities, and the weather—ever unpredictable and so often spectacular—make this tournament a perennial favorite of both golfers and golf fans alike.*

I always enjoyed the ambiance, as well as the opportunity to see old friends and make new ones. The competition was keen, and I came close to winning several times, finishing second in 1966 and 1971, and third in 1967. The final round that year proved dramatic—and bizarre. On the par-5 14th hole I was standing in the fairway tied for the lead with Jack Nicklaus. I decided to go for the green, and I hit a solid shot, but it ticked a branch on a massive pine and squirted out of bounds. I tried the same shot again but hit that same tree again, went out of bounds, and that ended my chances. That night a storm took down that offensive pine, a day too late.

I do not own that trophy, but I do own the next best thing: Pebble Beach Golf Links, which a group of partners and I purchased in 1999. These days I return to Pebble Beach for board meetings and also to consult on preparations for the 2010 U.S. Open. But mostly I come back to enjoy a few days of golf with good friends. Just like the old days."

—ARNOLD PALMER

"Pebble Beach has been a part of my life for many years. I have special memories of winning the AT&T in 2000 and the U.S. Open later that year. Combining beauty, history, and tradition, it is a truly special place."

—TIGER WOODS

"The Crosby was my first PGA Tour event. I Monday qualified, made my first cut, and earned my first paycheck. The AT&T Pro-Am is among the most significant tournaments in golf because it gives golfers on tour a chance to spend time with the individuals who make it all possible. I will continue to play as long as they will have me."

—PETER JACOBSEN

"As a child I watched the Pro-Am and was mesmerized by the extraordinary golf courses, the iconic figures, the great champions, and the camaraderie they shared. I have been blessed to be a part of this tradition, and for that I am eternally grateful. Dreams do come true."

—ANDY GARCIA

"My favorite memory from the tournament dates back to my first year, when I hit my approach on the 18th hole at Pebble Beach down onto the beach and managed to get up and down for par. You have to truly love golf to play in the wind and rain and 40-degree weather—and I do!"

—SAMUEL L. JACKSON

"If ever there was a place where the golf gods and humanity met, it has to be on the Monterey Peninsula. This event has defined what golf should be: a time and place to enjoy friends among some of the most spectacular scenery in the world."

—HALE IRWIN

"I have played in the tournament for the past ten years, and the honor, thrill, and excitement are the same every time. Every night I can only get about three hours sleep. My golfing buddy, Kevin James, explains it perfectly: 'It's like Christmas morning every day.'"

—RAY ROMANO

"I'm not quite good enough to play in the U.S. Amateur, so this is as big as it gets. I wait all year for that invitation to come in the mail, and to say I get butterflies in my stomach is an understatement. Quite simply, the AT&T at Pebble Beach is the Super Bowl for me."

—CHRIS O'DONNELL

"Nostalgia is something I deeply appreciate, and Bing Crosby's link to Pebble Beach is undeniably tethered forever. I feel his spirit and presence every time I step foot on the sacred sod."

—JIM NANTZ

Foreword

I FIRST EXPERIENCED the Crosby Clambake in the early 1950s—not as a player, but as a spectator. I was 21 years old and in the Army stationed at nearby Fort Ord, and a friend and I decided to go check out the action. The invitation-only clambake was held at the Monterey Peninsula Country Club for players and guests. My friend and I were neither, but we showed up anyway and told the guy at the door that we were working for Art Rosenbaum of the *San Francisco Chronicle*. The guy looked at us suspiciously—he could tell we were GIs by our shaved heads—but he let us in anyway. Once inside, we ate free food and drank free wine, hobnobbed with the golfers, and enjoyed the entertainment by the likes of Bob Hope, Rosemary Clooney, Phil Harris, and, of course, Bing Crosby.

At that time I did not play golf at all. I caddied as a kid at the the Orinda Country Club and Claremont Country Club in Oakland, California, but it wasn't until I was at Fort Ord that I took up the game. Friends and I would borrow clubs and play Pacific Grove, which at the time was a nine-holer. They charged something like fifty cents, and we would play all day.

In 1964 Bing kindly invited me to play in his tournament. I had taken part in a few one-day celebrity events, but nothing like the Crosby. I was paired with a pro named Stan Thirsk, and I was assigned the maximum handicap, which in those days was something like 14, even though I could not play to that. Still, the experience was unforgettable.

Over the years I suspect I have played the event as many times as anyone. The lowest my handicap ever dipped was 12, and unlike my friend Jack Lemmon, I even made the cut a few times. My most memorable shot occurred on the famous par-3 16th hole at Cypress Point. There was a delay, and the tee was all stacked up, so when it came my turn to hit, there were not only a bunch of spectators watching but also a couple other groups of celebrities and Tour pros. It does not get much more nerve-wracking, but I hit a four-wood to about two feet like it was no big thing.

The pro-am has grown from a little gathering into a big business, and yet it has managed to maintain the intimate feel and uniquely collegial spirit that sets this event apart from any other golf tournament in the world. This is a tribute to the hardworking volunteers, staff, and board members, a dedicated group with whom I am proud to be associated.

—CLINT EASTWOOD
CHAIRMAN
Monterey Peninsula Foundation

"If I were asked what single thing has given me the most gratification in my long and sometimes pedestrian career, I think I would have to say it is this tournament."

—BING CROSBY

Introduction

LIKE THE GOLF tournament itself, the souvenir program cover artwork has evolved beyond expectations. In those first few years that the Crosby Clambake was played on the Monterey Peninsula, the covers were fun but nothing exceptional. Then in 1950, a golf-loving local artist named Hank Ketcham, who had worked for Disney on movies including *Pinocchio* and *Bambi*, delivered an illustration showing a merry foursome traipsing up a fairway. That group did not include Dennis the Menace, the character Ketcham would introduce to the world the following year.

Hank became actively involved in the tournament, both as a regular pro-am player and also as a driving force behind the souvenir programs. In addition to contributing covers, he drew the course maps and enlisted a number of his comic strip colleagues; over the years the programs have included original artwork—always donated—by the likes of Lank Leonard (*Mickey Finn*), Gus Arriola (*Gordo*), Walt Kelly (*Pogo*), and Al Capp (*Li'l Abner*).

The Carmel area has always been very community oriented, and over the years a number of residents have generously given their time and talents to the Crosby Clambake program covers, notably Donald Teague, an esteemed illustrator and watercolorist, and Eldon Dedini, whose distinctive style graced the pages of the *New Yorker, Esquire*, and our humble tournament programs. Even after

he left Carmel and moved to Geneva, Switzerland, Hank Ketcham would make the annual trek back to play in the tournament. He eventually returned home to the Peninsula, and in later years, when he was no longer competing in the pro-am, Hank was a constant presence and could usually be found leaning up against a tree, pad in hand, sketching.

In 1990 the program cover featured a match between Dennis the Menace and Snoopy. *Peanuts* creator Charles Schulz became a fixture in the pro-am and a close friend of the family. "Sparky" contributed dozens of original works for the programs, each of which added humor, levity, and perspective to this unique annual gathering.

The focus of these works of art ranges from faces and places to the unpredictable weather, majestic landscapes, and unforgettable moments. In 1984 LeRoy Neiman created a painting commemorating Jerry Pate's hole in one at No. 16 at Cypress Point. Surrounding the scene are a collection of friends and our family, including Bing.

He had left us seven years earlier, but Bing was, and in many ways remains, a guiding spirit for the friendly little Clambake that's become the biggest and best golf tournament of its kind. Like each and every one of these program covers, the AT&T Pebble Beach National Pro-Am is a true original.

—KATHRYN, HARRY, NATHANIEL,
AND MARY FRANCES CROSBY

The 1940s

THE FIRST NATIONAL PRO-AMATEUR GOLF CHAMPIONSHIP SPONSORED BY BING CROSBY CONTESTED ON THE MONTEREY PENINSULA TOOK PLACE IN JANUARY 1947, THOUGH THE STORY BEGINS 13 YEARS EARLIER, IN THE SUMMER OF 1934. A FEW MONTHS AFTER BOBBY JONES, THE WORLD'S MOST FAMOUS GOLFER, HOSTED THE INAUGURAL GATHERING OF HIS "AUGUSTA NATIONAL INVITATION" TOURNAMENT, BING CROSBY, THE WORLD'S MOST FAMOUS ENTERTAINER, INVITED A GROUP OF CELEBRITY FRIENDS TO JOIN HIM FOR A FEW DAYS OF GOLF AND MERRIMENT ON THE NORTH SHORE OF LAKE TAHOE.

The Old Brockway Golf Course only had 12 holes, but it was plenty challenging—and made for a quicker trip back to the bar. Old Brockway became the playground of the golf-loving Rat Pack in the Sixties when Frank Sinatra owned the nearby Cal Neva resort, and legend holds that Dean Martin's predilection for playing holes 1, 2, 3, 8, and 9 so he could refill his drink even more expediently became known as the "Whiskey Run," the same name given to the five-hole loop of Nos. 1, 2, 3, 17, and 18 at Pebble Beach.

After a few years at Lake Tahoe, Crosby organized a more formal golf gathering in Rancho Santa Fe, California, just north of San Diego, where Crosby owned a home and was a partner, along with Jimmy Durante, Oliver Hardy, Pat O'Brien and others, in the grand opening of the sparkling new Del Mar Racetrack.

Crosby's vision was to pair professional golfers who wintered on the West Coast (and could use a few extra bucks to help make their way along the fledgling Tour) with amateurs drawn largely from Crosby's circle of celebrity friends and fellow members at the Lakeside Golf Club in Hollywood, where Crosby was the club champion five times.

Crosby had game. He learned to golf as a teenager, playing on days when he wasn't caddying for fifty cents a loop at the Downriver Golf Club in Spokane, Washington, though he did not play while a pre-law student at Gonzaga University. Crosby's legal aspirations ended when he got a gig fronting a local band, a career move that would soon lead him to Hollywood. It was while filming *The King of Jazz* in 1930 that Crosby picked up his sticks again, and in short order he whittled his handicap down to a two. For all his awards and accolades as an entertainer, Crosby was equally proud of having qualified for both the United States and British Amateur championships and scored 13 holes in one, highlighted by an ace at the famous 16th hole at Cypress Point.

The total purse for the pro-am that first year was $3,000, which Crosby staked himself, and the format for the team portion of the tournament was best ball, 18 holes a day, for two days. In a curious case of foreshadowing what would become known as "Crosby weather," the first day was washed out by torrential rains. To pass the time, a few of the contestants took to shooting ducks on the pond beside the 18th hole. When play resumed, Sam Snead won the pro portion of the rain-shortened event, along with the team competition with amateur partner George Lewis.

When Crosby (who carded an 87) presented Snead with the winner's check for just over $700,

Sam Snead and Ben Hogan   Julian P. Graham/Pebble Beach Company Lagorio Archives

the 24-year-old country boy from Virginia, in his first year on the Tour and fresh off his first victory at the Oakland Open, famously remarked, "If it's all the same to you, Mr. Crosby, I'd rather have the cash."

Any doubts Snead might have harbored over the viability of the event would prove to be unfounded, as the Crosby was here to stay.

Bing Crosby invented the celebrity pro-am and was the first star to attach his name to a Tour event. Forty years later, the PGA Tour schedule read like a lineup at a Friar's Club roast: Bing Crosby National Pro-Am, Bob Hope Desert Classic, Dean Martin Tucson Open, Jackie Gleason Inverrary Classic, Danny Thomas Memphis Classic, Andy Williams San Diego Open, Glen Campbell Los Angeles Open, Ed McMahon Quad Cities Open, Sammy Davis Jr. Greater Hartford Open.

The lucky invitees played hard both on the course and off. Crosby's backyard, conveniently located on the back nine, was party central, with the host mixing the drinks, grilling the food, and entertaining guests with song. The party was as much a part of the draw as the golf, and the closing night bash on the beach gave rise to the name "The Clambake," the moniker by which the event would be known for the next half century.

Masters champion Byron Nelson made the scene the second year, as did another young Texan who was scuffling to make it on Tour, Ben Hogan. Entered in the amateur field was a keen golfer who was new to Hollywood named Bob Hope. Babe Didrikson Zaharias played the following year, in 1939, and other notable amateurs to receive Bing's invitation included Zeppo Marx, Fred Astaire, and Mysterious Montague. One of the most curious characters in the annals of golf, Montague once bet Crosby that he could beat him playing with a baseball bat, a shovel, and a garden rake. The match is said to have ended after one hole when

Lloyd Mangrum   Julian P. Graham/Pebble Beach Company Lagorio Archives

Montague made birdie putting with the rake.

Snead repeated as champion in 1938, a title he would claim for a third time in 1941. The following year marked the end of the Clambake, as Crosby focused his time on raising money and morale in support of the war effort.

Following a four-year hiatus during World War II, the Clambake returned in January 1947. At the behest of *Monterey Herald* sports editor Ted Durein, Dan Searle, and other civic leaders seeking ways to jumpstart an economy hit hard by dwindling sardine production on Cannery Row, and with the support of Cam Puget, head professional at Monterey Peninsula Country

Club, Crosby agreed to move his party up the California coast to Pebble Beach.

The tournament expanded to 54 holes, with all golfers playing a different course for each of the three rounds: Cypress Point Club on Friday, Monterey Peninsula Country Club on Saturday, and Pebble Beach Golf Links on Sunday. To comply with PGA Tour policy that all tournaments have a minimum $10,000 purse, Crosby upped the ante out of his own pocket so that all proceeds went to charity; that year, donations were divided equally between the Sister Kenney Foundation for Infantile Paralysis and the Monterey Peninsula Community Chest.

The top six amateurs (with ties decided by a roll of dice) won Philco radios, with the winner receiving a console radio-phonograph combination. Crosby likely received the prizes as in-kind trade for the full-page advertisement on the inside back cover of the 16-page souvenir program, which promoted *"Philco Radio Time* starring Bing Crosby, Wednesday night at nine over ABC."

The scenery may have changed but the scene did not: golf by day, party by night, three days straight. The Clambake was such a hot ticket that Crosby offered a personal apology in the program:

We regret it was impossible to include all the amateurs who signified a desire to play, but the winter days are short and it's just impossible to move a field of more than 160 players around a golf course between daylight and dark. We hope all will appreciate our problem, and want them to know we appreciate their interest.

One amateur who did receive a standing invitation was Johnny Weissmuller. Playing in an adjoining fairway, the Olympic Gold medalist-cum-actor turned when he heard the host holler the name of the character Weissmuller famously portrayed on the silver screen. "Hey Tarzan," Crosby shouted after hitting a drive that stuck in a tree. "I've got a job for you!"

Sam Snead made a valiant run at a fourth victory but came up three strokes short of George Fazio and co-champion Ed Furgol, who eagled the 16th hole at Pebble Beach then made clutch pars on the home holes in a downpour to earn a share of the title. Snead had to have been pleasantly stunned to win the team competition with partner Roger Kelly, a decorated amateur golfer and professional drinker who started things off by throwing up in the bushes alongside the first tee. (Crosby may have been partly to blame for this given his tradition of gifting special edition fifths of liquor to each contestant . . . each day.)

The 1948 Clambake began with Bing receiving the title of honorary Chief of Police from the city of Monterey. "There is no place like the Peninsula in the world," Crosby said at the presentation ceremony. "This event will be a feature here for many more years to come."

Lloyd Mangrum, described by a local writer as "the competitive spirit and swell person with the nifty golf swing," thumped the field by five strokes, evidently unfazed by the effects of holding court into the wee hours at local watering holes the Blue Ox and Biff's El Estero.

Ben Hogan and partner Johnny Dawson took the 1948 team title, then Hogan returned in 1949 and refused to be denied. "When Old Blue Blades Hogan makes up his mind, it's just good night," said Crosby at the Sunday night banquet, "that's all, brother."

Seventeen days later, Hogan survived a harrowing head-on collision with a Greyhound bus. He spent two months in the hospital recuperating from a broken left ankle, broken collarbone, double-fracture of the pelvis, a chipped rib, and life-threatening blood clots. Doctors suggested Hogan might never walk again, much less play golf, certainly not competitively.

Hogan thought otherwise and had no intention of *not* defending his title at the Crosby Clambake.

1947

JANUARY 10–12

CYPRESS POINT CLUB
MONTEREY PENINSULA COUNTRY CLUB
PEBBLE BEACH GOLF LINKS

PROFESSIONALS

George Fazio	T1	68	70	75	213	$1,625
Ed Furgol	T1	72	69	72	213	$1,625
Lloyd Mangrum	T3	72	68	76	216	
Sam Snead	T3	76	70	70	216	
Newt Bassler	T3	71	74	71	216	

PRO-AM TEAMS

Sam Snead Roger Kelly	1	64	66	66	196
Al Zimmerman Bud Ward	T2	65	67	67	199
Newt Bassler F. A. Buck Hennekin	T2	65	66	68	199

Harrison Godwin, ARTIST

INVITATIONAL

$10,000 National Pro-Amateur

GOLF CHAMPIONSHIP

FOR CHARITY

Sponsored by
BING CROSBY

FRIDAY, JANUARY 10, 1947
CYPRESS POINT CLUB

☆   ☆

SATURDAY, JANUARY 11, 1947
MONTEREY PENINSULA
COUNTRY CLUB

☆   ☆

SUNDAY, JANUARY 12, 1947
PEBBLE BEACH

SOUVENIR
PROGRAM
Price 50 cents

BY HARRISON GODWIN

1948

JANUARY 9–11

CYPRESS POINT CLUB
MONTEREY PENINSULA COUNTRY CLUB
PEBBLE BEACH GOLF LINKS

PROFESSIONALS

Lloyd Mangrum	1	70	67	68	205	$2,000
Stan Leonard	2	71	67	72	210	
Ben Hogan	3	72	69	70	211	

PRO-AM TEAMS

Ben Hogan Johnny Dawson	1	70	63	64	197
Chandler Harper Warner Keeley	T2	67	64	68	199
Bobby Locke Frank Stranahan	T2	67	67	65	199
Lloyd Mangrum Bob Simmers	T2	68	66	65	199

Royden Martin, ARTIST

1949

JANUARY 14–16

CYPRESS POINT CLUB
MONTEREY PENINSULA COUNTRY CLUB
PEBBLE BEACH GOLF LINKS

PROFESSIONALS

Ben Hogan	1	70	68	70	208	$2,000
Jim Ferrier	2	69	70	71	210	
Jimmy Demaret	3	69	70	72	211	

PRO-AM TEAMS

Bill Nary	1	61	66	69	196
Francis "Lefty" O'Doul					
John Barnum	2	61	66	71	198
Harrison Goodwin					

Virgil Partch, ARTIST

EIGHTH ANNUAL
$10,000 INVITATIONAL
NATIONAL PRO-AMATEUR
GOLF CHAMPIONSHIP
Over 3 world famous courses on the
SCENIC
MONTEREY PENINSULA

JANUARY
14, 15, 16

Cypress Point Club

Monterey Peninsula
Country Club

Pebble Beach

Souvenir Program ☆ Fifty Cents

LARRY CROSBY, General Chairman
MAURIE LUXFORD, Tournament Director
DAN SEARLE, Asst. Tournament Director

Sponsored By
Bing Crosby

The 1950s

S O COVETED WAS A CLAMBAKE INVITE THAT ONE ASPIRING INVITEE TOOK TO SKYWRITING TO PLEAD HIS CASE. CROSBY SOUGHT RESPITE FROM THE CONSTANT CALLS AND EARNEST APPEALS BY RETIRING TO HIS HOME IN BAJA, MEXICO, WHERE HE COULD CRAFT THE LIST IN PEACE. HE WAS THE SOLE ARBITER OF NOT ONLY WHO PLAYED BUT ALSO OF HANDICAPS. CROSBY DID NOT SUFFER SANDBAGGING, AND HE PERSONALLY EVALUATED EACH AMATEUR'S ABILITIES AND ASSIGNED STROKES ACCORDINGLY. THE HOST DID ENJOY HIS PICK OF PRO PARTNERS, THOUGH FIVE STROKES SHORT WAS THE CLOSEST CROSBY EVER GOT TO WINNING HIS OWN TOURNAMENT.

Among the annual highlights were the Thursday clinic and Sunday night party. Staged on the second tee at Pebble Beach and drawing crowds of well over a thousand, a handful of top pros took part in the clinic, which offered "a million-dollar lesson for a buck," with all proceeds, as ever, going to charity.

The banquet featured top entertainment of the day, including a star turn at the mic for Bing. Sharing a table and a few laughs with Crosby at the 1950 soiree was Ben Hogan, who made good on his vow to return from his near-death experience and defend his title. Hogan finished T19 in inclement weather that nagged his injuries, nine shots back of the quartet of co-champions: Sam Snead, Smiley Quick, Jack Burke Jr., and Dave Douglas.

More than 20,000 spectators came out for the 1951 event, though few could have expected the winner to be a cattle rancher from Texas. Four years removed from the Pro Tour, Byron Nelson moseyed out of retirement to beat Dr. Cary Middlecoff by three strokes.

The one-liner of the week came courtesy of Crosby favorite Phil Harris, the bandleader who never met a joke or a drink he did not like and listed his home course as the Jack Daniels Country Club. After snaking in a 90-foot putt at the 17th hole that helped clinch the team title, Harris turned to the host and quipped, "How about that, Bing. Ain't this a helluva blow to clean living?"

Bob Hope nearly took the title in 1952, finishing a shot back with pro partner Jimmy Demaret. Hope did his part at the par-5, 550-yard 14th hole when, hitting his third shot from behind a stand of trees 200 yards from the green, he sliced—intentionally or not—a beauty that rolled up onto the green just an inch from the pin.

That year the Crosby topped $100,000 donated to charity. It also marked the year of the "Big Blow," when Crosby weather arrived with a vengeance. Battling wicked winds, Middlecoff complained to Peter Hay, the Pebble Beach pro, that the ball would not stay on a tee. "Sure, and show me in the rule book where it says you have to tee up the ball," barked the Scotsman. "Now, get out there and play."

The field grew to 96 teams in 1953, and the format changed with the players alternating courses, half each at Cypress Point and Monterey Peninsula Country Club on Friday and Saturday, with the low 60 teams advancing to the finale at Pebble Sunday. Lloyd Mangrum bested his tournament scoring record by one to claim his second title, while 1940 Clambake champion Ed "Porky" Oliver infamously carded a 16 at the famous par-3 16th hole at Cypress Point.

Bing Crosby
Julian P. Graham/Pebble Beach Company Lagorio Archives

In 1954 Dutch Harrison arrived on the final tee of the final round with a comfy three-stroke lead, then scrambled home with a double bogey to eke out a win. The following year, the future of golf was on display at the Thursday clinic as advertised by this item in the souvenir program:

Another step forward in the mechanized age is being witnessed at this tournament in the power-operated golf cart that not only carries bags but gives the user an assist.

Cartoonist, Carmel resident, and frequent Clambake participant Hank Ketcham of *Dennis the Menace* fame designed that program, a year that saw Dr. Cary Middlecoff win the first of his back-to-back Crosby titles. His second win in 1956

came in what proved to be the last Crosby in which Bing himself would play. His hand-picked partner was Ben Hogan, also playing in his last Clambake. The weather was so miserable that Crosby offered Hogan relief from the rain and invited him into his home off the 13th hole. Ever the competitor, Hogan soldiered on and slogged in with an 81.

The following year, Jay Hebert, an ex-Marine who saw action at Iwo Jima, held on for a two-stroke victory that dashed the hopes of a three-peat for runner-up Middlecoff.

Big changes marked the 1958 Crosby Clambake. Bing was a newlywed, having married Kathryn Grant the previous October. The tournament expanded to 72 holes, and the purse jumped from $15,000 to $50,000 thanks to Bud Gould, the president of the Murray Corporation of Detroit, Michigan, who bought the broadcasting and film rights to the event so as to advertise his company's Easy Washing Machine equipment. For the first time, the National Pro-Amateur Golf Championship was broadcast on national television. Billy Casper won the tournament, which saw the Crosby debut of a young, handsome, made-for-TV star named Arnold Palmer.

In 1959 Art Wall started the final round with a four-stroke lead and promptly birdied three of the first four holes. Standing on the 16th tee five shots clear of the field, Wall notched consecutive bogeys while Gene Littler birdied both to shave the lead to one. Wall limped home with a 41 on the back nine, but that was good enough for a two-stroke win after Littler hooked his approach into a watery grave, reinforcing the reputation of the 18th hole at Pebble Beach as the greatest finishing hole in all of golf.

1950

CYPRESS POINT CLUB
MONTEREY PENINSULA COUNTRY CLUB
PEBBLE BEACH GOLF LINKS

PROFESSIONALS

Jack Burke Jr.	T1	75	67	72	214	$1,237
Dave Douglas	T1	71	73	70	214	$1,237
Sam Snead	T1	69	72	73	214	$1,237
Smiley Quick	T1	72	69	73	214	$1,237

PRO-AM TEAMS

| Ralph Blomquist | T1 | 69 | 64 | 68 | 201 |
| Bud Moe | | | | | |

| Marty Furgol | T1 | 68 | 64 | 69 | 201 |
| Don Edwards | | | | | |

9th

NATIONAL PRO-AMATEUR GOLF CHAMPIONSHIP

JANUARY 13
CYPRESS POINT

☆

JANUARY 14
MONTEREY PENINSULA
COUNTRY CLUB

☆

JANUARY 15
PEBBLE BEACH

☆

LARRY CROSBY
General Chairman

MAURIE LUXFORD
Tournament Director

DAN SEARLE
Asst. Tournament Director

☆

$10,000.00
ANNUAL
INVITATIONAL

☆

SOUVENIR PROGRAM
FIFTY CENTS

Sponsored by

Bing Crosby

1951

JANUARY 12–14

CYPRESS POINT CLUB
MONTEREY PENINSULA COUNTRY CLUB
PEBBLE BEACH GOLF LINKS

PROFESSIONALS

Byron Nelson	1	71	67	71	209	$2,000
Cary Middlecoff	2	76	67	69	212	
Ed Furgol	T3	75	70	68	213	
George Fazio	T3	71	71	71	213	
Julius Boros	T3	72	72	69	213	

PRO-AM TEAMS

E. J. "Dutch" Harrison Phil Harris	1	69	60	67	196
Joe Kirkwood Jr. Ben Gage	2	67	64	67	198

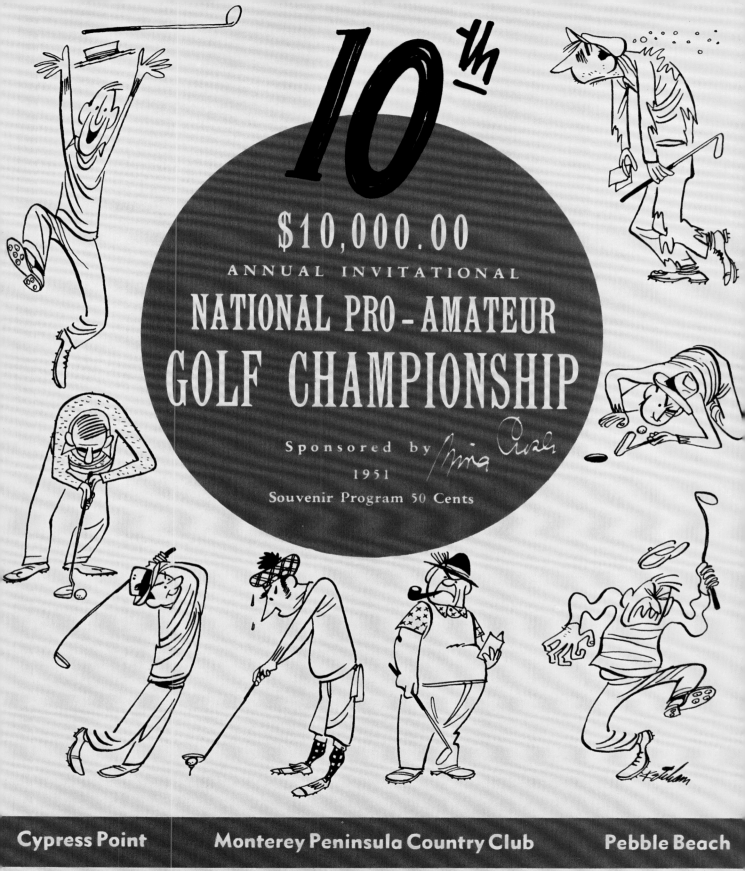

10th

$10,000.00
ANNUAL INVITATIONAL
NATIONAL PRO-AMATEUR
GOLF CHAMPIONSHIP

Sponsored by *Bing Crosby*

1951

Souvenir Program 50 Cents

Cypress Point   **Monterey Peninsula Country Club**   **Pebble Beach**

JANUARY 12th-13th-14th

1952

JANUARY 11–13

CYPRESS POINT CLUB
MONTEREY PENINSULA COUNTRY CLUB
PEBBLE BEACH GOLF LINKS

PROFESSIONALS

Jimmy Demaret	1	74	71	145	$2,000
Art Bell	2	75	72	147	
Doug Ford	3	78	70	148	

PRO-AM TEAMS

Art Bell William Hoelle	T1	70	63	133
Bob Toski Dr. Bob Knutson	T1	68	65	133

Bill O'Malley, ARTIST

1953

JANUARY 9–11

CYPRESS POINT CLUB
MONTEREY PENINSULA COUNTRY CLUB
PEBBLE BEACH GOLF LINKS

PROFESSIONALS

Lloyd Mangrum	1	67	66	71	204	$2,000
Julius Boros	2	69	67	72	208	
Lawson Little	3	70	70	69	209	

PRO-AM TEAMS

Cary Middlecoff Ed Crowley	T1	63	65	62	190
Gene Webb Col. I. F. Wintermute	T1	61	63	66	190
Paul Runyon Bob Vaillancourt	T1	62	61	67	190

Marty Crail, PHOTOGRAPHER

12th
ANNUAL

$10,000.00
Invitational
National Pro-Amateur

GOLF CHAMPIONSHIP

Sponsored by

Bing Crosby

JANUARY 9-10-11, 1953

Cypress Point ★ Monterey Peninsula Country Club ★ Pebble Beach

Souvenir Program—Fifty Cents

1954

JANUARY 15–17

CYPRESS POINT CLUB
MONTEREY PENINSULA COUNTRY CLUB
PEBBLE BEACH GOLF LINKS

PROFESSIONALS

E. J. "Dutch" Harrison	1	71	68	71	210	$2,000
Jimmy Demaret	2	73	68	70	211	
Tommy Bolt	3	71	70	71	212	

PRO-AM TEAMS

Bud Ward Harvie Ward	T1	64	67	62	193
Walter Burkemo Francis "Lefty" O'Doul	T1	66	62	65	193
Art Wall Jr. Gene Littler	T1	62	65	66	193
Doug Ford Monty Moncrief	T1	66	62	65	193

Al Wiseman, ARTIST

- cypress point
- monterey peninsula country club
- pebble beach

january 15, 16, 17, 1954

national pro-amateur golf championship 13th

souvenir program .50

sponsored by

Bing Crosby

all proceeds for charity

1955

JANUARY 14–16

CYPRESS POINT CLUB
MONTEREY PENINSULA COUNTRY CLUB
PEBBLE BEACH GOLF LINKS

PROFESSIONALS

Cary Middlecoff	1	69	69	71	209	$2,500
Paul Maguire	T2	68	75	70	213	
Julius Boros	T2	70	71	72	213	

PRO-AM TEAMS

| Byron Nelson Ed Lowery | 1 | 64 | 68 | 63 | 195 |
| Cary Middlecoff Ed Crowley | 2 | 66 | 64 | 66 | 196 |

14th

NATIONAL PRO-AMATEUR GOLF CHAMPIONSHIP

1955 - SOUVENIR PROGRAM - FIFTY CENTS

1956

JANUARY 13–15

CYPRESS POINT CLUB
MONTEREY PENINSULA COUNTRY CLUB
PEBBLE BEACH GOLF LINKS

PROFESSIONALS

Cary Middlecoff	1	66	68	68	202	$2,500
Mike Souchak	2	64	71	72	207	
Bill Ogden	T3	68	69	74	211	
Bob Rosburg	T3	69	65	77	211	

PRO-AM TEAMS

Ralph Blomquist George Galios	1	61	60	67	188
Donald Whitt Dr. Ed Lambert	2	62	64	65	191

Jack Crosby & Hendry Sargent

NATIONAL PRO-AMA
championship

15th annual
MONTEREY
Jan. 12-15 1956

Hendry Sargent
Zack Crosby

SOUVENIR PROGRAM $1.00

1957

JANUARY 11–13

CYPRESS POINT CLUB
MONTEREY PENINSULA COUNTRY CLUB
PEBBLE BEACH GOLF LINKS

PROFESSIONALS

Jay Hebert	1	74	69	70	213	$2,500
Cary Middlecoff	2	76	67	72	215	
Stan Leonard	3	68	74	74	216	

PRO-AM TEAMS

Cary Middlecoff	1	62	59	66	187
Ed Crowley					
Jay Hebert	2	65	63	68	196
Roger Kelly					

16th

NATIONAL PRO-AMATEUR

Golf Championship

SPONSORED BY BING CROSBY

1957 · SOUVENIR PROGRAM · ONE DOLLAR

1958

JANUARY 9–12

CYPRESS POINT CLUB
MONTEREY PENINSULA COUNTRY CLUB
PEBBLE BEACH GOLF LINKS

PROFESSIONALS

Billy Casper	1	71	66	69	71	277	$4,000
Dave Marr	2	69	70	70	72	281	
Ken Venturi	T3	68	74	70	72	284	
Dow Finsterwald	T3	73	67	69	75	284	
Jack Burke Jr.	T3	72	68	71	73	284	

PRO-AM TEAMS

| Jay Hebert Roger Kelly | 1 | 65 | 65 | 64 | 66 | 260 |
| Billy Casper Bob Reynolds | 2 | 67 | 61 | 68 | 65 | 261 |

Colden Whitman, COVER DESIGN

Hoagy Carmichael
Ben Hogan
Stan Searle
Ed. Sines
Cary Middlecoff
Bob Rosburg
Eddie Lowery
Doug Ford
"Bones" Hamilton

Glenn Graham
Mahlon Rucker
Jay Bedsworth
Byron Nelson
Ed "Bump" Schmidt
Sunny O'Keefe
Jim Turnesa
Jay Hebert
Lionel Hebert
Sammy McLarnin

Lenny Crosby
Bud Ward
Bob Littler
Coleman
Henry Puget
George
Jackie Jensen
Bud Giles
Ted Durein
S ? B Morse
Lawrie Ruxford
Thoms. H.J. Brown
J. Harrison
Tommy Bolt E. Co.
Dewing Morgan
Ed Crawley
Winiger
Borden
Freeman
Walter Burkemo
Howard Hill
R. McCrudy
Ken Venturi

17th

NATIONAL PRO-AMATEUR GOLF CHAMPIONSHIP
SPONSORED BY BING CROSBY

1958

SOUVENIR PROGRAM   **ONE DOLLAR**

1959

JANUARY 15–18

CYPRESS POINT CLUB
MONTEREY PENINSULA COUNTRY CLUB
PEBBLE BEACH GOLF LINKS

PROFESSIONALS

Art Wall Jr.	1	69	65	70	75	279	$4,000
Jimmy Demaret	T2	74	67	70	73	281	
Gene Littler	T2	73	67	71	73	281	

PRO-AM TEAMS

Art Wall Jr. Charles Coe	1	65	60	62	65	252
Doug Ford Art Anderson	2	66	64	64	63	257

Eldon Dedini, ARTIST

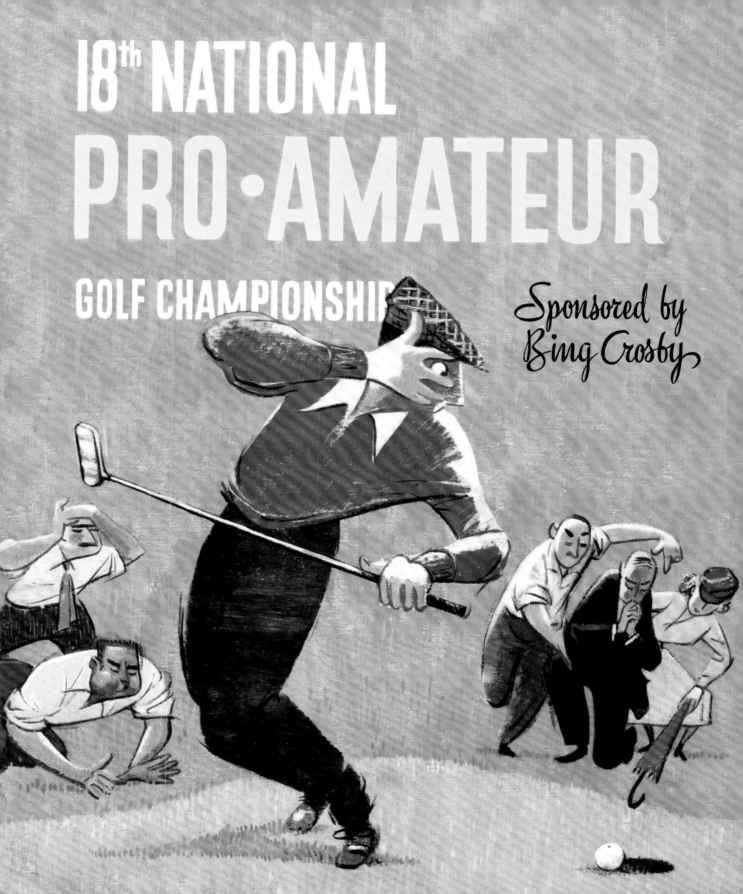

18th NATIONAL PRO·AMATEUR

GOLF CHAMPIONSHIP

Sponsored by Bing Crosby

MONTEREY · JAN · 15, 16, 17, 18 · '59 · SOUVENIR PROGRAM $1.00 · PROCEEDS TO CHARITY

The 1960s

THE STARS SHINED BRIGHTER THAN EVER IN THE '60S. MAKING THE SCENE WERE SUCH HOLLYWOOD LUMINARIES AS DEAN MARTIN, SEAN CONNERY, BURT LANCASTER, JAMES GARNER, DESI ARNAZ, FRANKIE AVALON, BOB NEWHART, FRED MACMURRAY, AND FORREST TUCKER, WHO TEAMED WITH PRO CHARLIE SIFFORD. AFTER MISSING A PUTT THAT LOOKED TO BE GOING IN, THE GALLERY GROANED IN UNISON. "WHAT'S SO TRAGIC?" SAID THE TV STAR. "I DON'T DO THIS FOR A LIVING!" SIFFORD STEPPED UP, EYED A TRICKY PUTT FOR PAR, COOLY BURIED IT IN THE CUP, THEN TURNED TO TUCKER AND THE CROWD AND SAID, "YES, BUT I DO."

Drenching rains and howling winds marked the 1960 Clambake. "Some of the golfers hired two caddies—one to pack the bag and the other to hang on to," wrote a local scribe. "Fat caddies who could stand against the wind were in great demand." Only 17 pros managed to match or better par—and 15 of those played the Monterey Peninsula Country Club. San Franciscan Ken Venturi shot to the top of the leaderboard following an impressive 68 at Cypress Point on Saturday, then held on to win by three strokes despite a final round 77. Mother Nature was not in a good mood, but Mother (Ethyl) Venturi was over the moon after trudging along each and every one of the 72 holes to watch her boy win. Olympic swimming champion Johnny Weissmuller, no stranger to water, declared, "I have never been so wet in my life."

Another local boy made good the following year when San Francisco native and former Stanford University star Bob Rosburg won the 1961 event. Rosburg probably did not give himself much of a chance considering he started Sunday seven strokes back and had twice before held the final round lead, only to balloon with a closing 77 in 1956 and an ugly 81 two years later. But this day, Rosburg rolled in a 14-footer for birdie on the last hole to nip Roberto de Vicenzo and Dave Ragan by a stroke.

The odds of anything happening just once in the long history of the tournament are slim. To wit, in 69 years there have been 68 holes in one. And yet, 1962 remains the one and only time a round was scuttled due to snow. It was a sight not seen in forty years: a blanket of white covering the peninsula. Golfers awaiting word of if and when (and how?!) they would play the final round were seen putting snowballs on the practice green. When play resumed on Monday, Doug Ford bested Joe Campbell in a sudden-death playoff. (A few rungs down the leaderboard, tied for twenty-third, was a promising rookie named Jack Nicklaus.) As memorable as the snow itself was Jimmy Demaret's famous remark, "I know I got loaded last night, but how did I end up in Squaw Valley?"

Leaving nothing to chance, Bing Crosby invited two priests to play in the tournament the following year. It worked. The weather was perfectly pleasant, and in one of the tightest finishes in tournament history, Billy Casper survived late charges from Gary Player, who missed a birdie putt to tie; Bob Duden, who three-putted the 18th green; and Nicklaus, who uncharacteristically missed a makeable six-foot putt to force a playoff.

That year, Arnold Palmer arrived at the Crosby riding a streak of 47 consecutive tournaments

Tournament Marshals   Julian P. Graham/Pebble Beach Company Lagorio Archives

in the money; however, that streak ended on Saturday. After his tee shot at the 17th hole at Pebble Beach flew the green and appeared to disappear into the ocean, Palmer invoked the lost ball rule and re-teed. But when marshals located his first ball on the rocks behind the 18th tee, Palmer proceeded to play the original ball. Officials ruled that he had abandoned his first ball by hitting the second and disqualified Palmer.

Palmer must have felt snakebit when, the following year—again at the 17th hole at Pebble, and again in the third round—Palmer launched his tee shot long and into a pool of shallow water on the rocks, an area that local rules deemed part of the course back in the day. With a national television audience and a stray Irish Setter looking on, Palmer struggled to find his way back to dry land. Quick-witted television commentator Jimmy Demaret noted, "His nearest drop is Honolulu." Palmer took a 9 on the hole and missed the cut by one stroke.

Also missing the cut was an amateur playing in his first Clambake: Clint Eastwood. Eastwood had joked that the reason he had not previously been asked to play was that maybe Crosby did not like cowboys. When Clint's invitation finally arrived, it carried a postscript from Bing: *P.S. By the way, I do like cowboys.*

The record does not show whether the fair-weather priests got the call to return in 1964, though pro Tony Lema sought divine intervention on his own by serving mass at the Carmel Mission on the morning of the final round. And while it did not seem to help—he shot 76—it was good enough to give Champagne Tony the title by three.

Bruce Crampton of Australia became the first foreign winner of the Crosby when, in 1965, he vanquished a pack of challengers that included defending champion Lema and Nicklaus. Crampton gave credit for his victory to Nicklaus, who, perhaps regrettably, offered Crampton a pre-tournament tip on the driving range. In 1966 Don Massengale earned his first Tour victory in dramatic fashion with a clutch birdie putt on the final hole to edge Arnold Palmer by a stroke.

Phil Harris, James Garner, Arnold Palmer

That year marked the Crosby Clambake's silver anniversary—or so Bing thought until an astute sportswriter pointed out that there had been six tournaments in Rancho Santa Fe, not the five that had been printed in the souvenir programs year after year for going on two decades. Larry Crosby, the longtime tournament chairman (and Bing's brother) copped to accidentally omitting 1942 and made sure the winners were duly noted in future editions.

Spyglass Hill Golf Course joined the Crosby rotation in 1967. So impressed—and intimidated—was the host by the Robert Trent Jones design that Crosby went on record saying, "I'll give Jack Nicklaus one practice round there and bet he can't shoot 72." Nicklaus carded a 70 in his practice round and for years to come would proudly display on his wall at home the personal check he received—for five dollars—autographed by Bing Crosby. After Saturday's gale-force winds resulted in suspension of play for, amazingly, only the third time in tournament history, the Golden Bear romped, birdieing five of the last seven holes on Sunday en route to a back nine 31 and his first Crosby championship.

Final round challenger Arnold Palmer came to the 14th hole just one stroke back—until his approach shot smacked a tree and ricocheted out

of bounds. Down but not out, Palmer reloaded, only to see his encore plunk the same tree and also carom out of bounds. Palmer carded a quadruple-bogey 9 on the hole and finished in third place. In what could only be chalked up to karma, a squall blew through later that night and toppled the offending tree.

Billy Casper was poised to win his third Crosby and thirty-fifth Tour victory in 1968 until journeyman Johnny Pott chipped in from off the green to take the title. The next year saw yet another local claim the winner's check. George Archer's first-place take of $24,950 represented a hefty raise over his first Crosby earnings: in 1957, the 17-year-old from nearby Gilroy caddied for host Pebble Beach professional Art Bell. "I went home with $50," said Archer, "after expenses."

The lasting legacy of the 1969 Crosby would prove to be the debut of Jack Lemmon. A major star with one Academy Award and three nominations already to his name, Lemmon often claimed he would trade an Oscar just to make the cut at the Crosby. His pursuit got off to an inauspicious start, as evidenced by television broadcaster Jim McKay's classic call: "And now here's Jack Lemmon, about to hit that all-important eighth shot."

Champagne Tony Lema
William C. Brooks/Pebble Beach Company Lagorio Archives

1960

JANUARY 21–24

CYPRESS POINT CLUB
MONTEREY PENINSULA COUNTRY CLUB
PEBBLE BEACH GOLF LINKS

PROFESSIONALS

Ken Venturi	1	70	71	68	77	286	$4,000
Julius Boros	T2	73	71	72	73	289	
Tommy Jacobs	T2	70	74	70	75	289	

PRO-AM TEAMS

Bud Ward	1	70	63	63	66	262
Bob Silvestri						
Julius Boros	T2	67	64	64	70	265
Don Schwab						
Ken Venturi	T2	65	66	65	69	265
Harvie Ward						

Runyan & Whitman, PROGRAM DESIGN

19TH NATIONAL PRO-AMATEUR GOLF CHAMPIONSHIP

Sponsored
by
BING
CROSBY

SOUVENIR
PROGRAM
$1.00
PROCEEDS
TO
CHARITY

JAN.
21, 22, 23, 24
1960
MONTEREY

IT'S LEAP YEAR—
SO THE GIRLS TAKE OVER

1961

CYPRESS POINT CLUB
MONTEREY PENINSULA COUNTRY CLUB
PEBBLE BEACH GOLF LINKS

PROFESSIONALS

Bob Rosburg	1	69	67	74	72	282	$5,300
Dave Ragan	T2	68	71	70	74	283	
Roberto deVicenzo	T2	72	66	70	75	283	

PRO-AM TEAMS

Wes Ellis	1	63	62	60	67	252
Frank Tatum Jr.						
Dow Finsterwald	2	60	64	63	67	254
Fred Kammer Jr.						

20th NATIONAL PRO-AMATEUR GOLF CHAMPIONSHIP

MONTEREY · JANUARY 19-20-21-22, 1961 · SOUVENIR PROGRAM $1.00 · PROCEEDS TO CHARITY

SPONSORED BY BING CROSBY

1962

JANUARY 18–21

CYPRESS POINT CLUB
MONTEREY PENINSULA COUNTRY CLUB
PEBBLE BEACH GOLF LINKS

PROFESSIONALS

Doug Ford*	1	70	73	69	74	286	$5,300
Joe Campbell	2	67	71	72	76	286	
Phil Rodgers	3	67	75	72	74	288	

*playoff

PRO-AM TEAMS

Bob McCallister Albie Pearson	1	59	64	62	70	255
Stan Leonard Dr. Bud Taylor	T2	62	68	64	67	261
Dow Finsterwald Fred Kammer Jr.	T2	65	65	65	66	261

1963

JANUARY 17–20

CYPRESS POINT CLUB
MONTEREY PENINSULA COUNTRY CLUB
PEBBLE BEACH GOLF LINKS

PROFESSIONALS

Billy Casper	1	73	65	73	74	285	$5,300
Bob Rosburg	T2	71	74	70	71	286	
Dave Hill	T2	68	69	76	73	286	
Art Wall Jr.	T2	71	71	72	72	286	
Gary Player	T2	73	69	70	74	286	
Jack Nicklaus	T2	71	69	76	70	286	

PRO-AM TEAMS

Doug Sanders	1	64	65	62	66	257
Lloyd Pitzer						
Bob Duden	T2	66	63	63	68	260
Ted Gleichmann						
Tommy Jacobs	T2	69	62	65	64	260
Wheeler Farish Jr.						

22ND NATIONAL PRO-AMATEUR GOLF
CHAMPIONSHIP JAN. 17 · 18 · 19 · 20 · 1963

SPONSORED BY BING CROSBY · PROCEEDS TO CHARITY · SOUVENIR PROGRAM $1.00

1964

JANUARY 16–19

CYPRESS POINT CLUB
MONTEREY PENINSULA COUNTRY CLUB
PEBBLE BEACH GOLF LINKS

PROFESSIONALS

Tony Lema	1	70	68	70	76	284	$5,800
Gay Brewer	T2	76	68	70	73	287	
Bo Wininger	T2	69	73	70	75	287	

PRO-AM TEAMS

Mike Fetchick Charles Seaver	1	58	65	66	69	258
Tony Lema Father John Durkin	2	63	60	66	70	259

Runyan & Whitman PROGRAM DESIGN

23 RD NATIONAL PRO-AMATEUR GOLF CHAMPIONSHIP

SPONSORED BY BING CROSBY JAN. 16·17·18·19·1964
SOUVENIR PROGRAM $1.00 · PROCEEDS TO CHARITY

1965

JANUARY 21–24

CYPRESS POINT CLUB
MONTEREY PENINSULA COUNTRY CLUB
PEBBLE BEACH GOLF LINKS

PROFESSIONALS

Bruce Crampton	1	75	67	73	69	284	$7,500
Tony Lema	2	71	65	79	72	287	
Billy Casper	T3	70	70	76	72	288	
Jack Nicklaus	T3	72	68	77	71	288	

PRO-AM TEAMS

George Bayer	T1	65	67	61	67	260
Morgan Barofsky						
George Archer	T1	66	65	63	66	260
Nelson Cullenward						

Runyan & Whitman PROGRAM DESIGN

NATIONAL PRO AMATEUR GOLF CHAMPIONSHIP

TOTAL PURSE $84,500.00

SPONSORED BY BING CROSBY
JANUARY 21st - 22nd - 23rd - 24th, 1965
SOUVENIR PROGRAM $1.00
PROCEEDS TO CHARITY

24th CROSBY

1966

JANUARY 20–23

CYPRESS POINT CLUB
MONTEREY PENINSULA COUNTRY CLUB
PEBBLE BEACH GOLF LINKS

PROFESSIONALS

Don Massengale	1	70	67	76	70	283	$11,000
Arnold Palmer	2	70	70	73	71	284	
Billy Martindale	T3	72	71	69	73	285	
Al Geiberger	T3	68	74	67	76	285	

PRO-AM TEAMS

Chuck Courtney	1	64	66	63	62	255*
John Moler						
Billy Martindale	2	63	62	61	69	255
Bob Roos Jr.						

*playoff

Colden Whitman ARTIST

JANUARY 20-21-22-23, 1966 • TOTAL PURSE $104,500 • SOUVENIR PROGRAM $1.00 • PROCEEDS TO CHARITY

1967

JANUARY 19–22

CYPRESS POINT CLUB
PEBBLE BEACH GOLF LINKS
SPYGLASS HILL GOLF COURSE

PROFESSIONALS

Jack Nicklaus	1	69	73	74	68	284	$16,000
Billy Casper	2	72	74	69	74	289	
Arnold Palmer	3	74	75	67	75	291	

PRO-AM TEAMS

Mike Souchak Frank Souchak	1	65	61	66	67	259
Chuck Courtney John Moler	T2	65	68	67	62	262
Ted Makalena Paul Spengler	T2	65	62	66	69	262
Al Geiberger Lew Leis	T2	63	67	64	68	262

Runyan & Whitman, PROGRAM DESIGN

BING'S 26TH NATIONAL PRO-AMATEUR GOLF CHAMPIONSHIP

SPONSORED BY BING CROSBY   JANUARY 19·20·21·22·1967   PROCEEDS TO CHARITY

1968

JANUARY 11–14

CYPRESS POINT CLUB
PEBBLE BEACH GOLF LINKS
SPYGLASS HILL GOLF COURSE

PROFESSIONALS

Johnny Pott*	1	70	71	71	73	285	$16,000
Billy Casper	T2	73	69	73	70	285	
Bruce Devlin	T2	73	69	73	70	285	

*playoff

PRO-AM TEAMS

| Johnny Pott
Virgil Sherrill | 1 | 59 | 66 | 67 | 61 | 253 |
| Billy Casper
Bob Dickson | 2 | 66 | 63 | 65 | 63 | 257 |

BING'S 27th PRO-AM

JAN. 11-12-13-14, 1968
OFFICIAL PROGRAM $1.00

1969

CYPRESS POINT CLUB
PEBBLE BEACH GOLF LINKS
SPYGLASS HILL GOLF COURSE

PROFESSIONALS

George Archer	1	72	68	72	71	283	$25,000
Bob Dickson	T2	73	69	74	68	284	
Dale Douglass	T2	71	69	70	74	284	
Howie Johnson	T2	71	69	71	73	284	

PRO-AM TEAMS

Bob Dickson Jack Ging	1	65	63	65	64	257
Billy Casper Mike Bonnallack	T2	61	65	67	65	258
Gene Littler John Moler	T2	68	64	63	63	258
Tom Nieporte Richard Remsen	T2	65	64	65	64	258
Tom Shaw Richard Crane	T2	62	61	68	67	258

THE 28TH

BING CROSBY

NATIONAL PRO-AM

JANUARY 23, 24, 25, 26, 1969

SOUVENIR PROGRAM ONE DOLLAR

The 1970s

THE '70S PROVIDED SOME OF THE GREATEST DISPLAYS OF GOLF ALONG WITH SOME OF THE WORST DISPLAYS OF FASHION. POLYESTER INEXPLICABLY BECAME EN VOGUE, OFTEN IN ELECTRIC COLORS AND FRENETIC PRINTS THAT WOULD CAUSE A CHAMELEON TO EXPLODE. THE FAD WAS REGRETTABLE, BUT THE PHOTOS ARE HILARIOUS.

Cited as one of only three national tournaments—the National Open, the National Amateur, and the National Pro-Amateur—the Crosby Clambake remained the biggest and best party in golf. Bidding for his second Crosby, Jack Nicklaus went out in 30 on Sunday at Pebble Beach and closed with a round of 65, but front-runner Bert Yancey, jangling a voodoo bracelet and tending to his own business, shot a 3-under-par 69 for a one-shot victory over Nicklaus. San Francisco 49ers quarterback John Brodie, who later in life would go on to win on the Senior Tour, took the Pro-Am with partner Bob Rosburg.

Arnold Palmer's year looked to be 1971—finally. After a decade of near misses and hard luck, Arnie and his Army made a trademark Sunday charge. Palmer chipped-in for eagle at the 2nd hole to catch young Tom Shaw, a sight for sore eyes in a bright green turtleneck and brighter yellow slacks, in homage to his alma mater, the University of Oregon. But the rain stayed away on a day that Palmer declared the calmest he had ever seen it at Pebble Beach in January. Shaw carded a 32 on the front, while Palmer faltered with bogeys at the 5th, 7th, and 9th holes, but it wasn't over yet. Shaw left the door open after missing par putts at Nos. 17 and 18, but once again Palmer could not seal the deal and had to settle for second. Highlighting the amateur field was astronaut Alan Shepard, who

played out of the Fra Mauro Valley Country Club—so named for the lunar landing site of Apollo 14.

A second consecutive year marked by exceptional weather made for ideal scoring conditions in 1972. On Thursday Larry Mowry shot a course record 69 at Spyglass Hill. On Friday Johnny Miller and Herb Hooper bested that short-lived record by a stroke. On Saturday Dan Sikes and Ken Towns each shot 66 to rewrite the Spyglass record book once more, while over at Pebble Beach Rod Funseth stole everybody's thunder with a course record 64. In the end it came down to Miller and Nicklaus, both of whom tried to give the tournament away. Miller hit what, by all accounts, was one of the worst shots in Crosby history when he shanked a seven-iron at the 16th hole, then Nicklaus generously three-putted the 17th green from 35 feet. The two finished in a tie, which Nicklaus broke with a long birdie putt on the first hole of the sudden-death playoff.

Later that summer Nicklaus returned to Pebble Beach and won the U.S. Open. The following January he claimed his third consecutive Tour title on the peninsula by defending his crown at the 1973 Crosby. Bing was hospitalized with pleurisy, so his good friend Bob Hope filled in as host. "It's great to be here," said Hope in welcoming the players, "to play this benefit for Jack Nicklaus." Lanny Wadkins, the 1970 U.S.

Locke de Bretteville and Johnny Miller, center   William C. Brooks/Pebble Beach Company Lagorio Archives

Amateur champion, climbed into contention thanks to 18 birdies in the first three days, then faded down the stretch with a final round 82. Raymond Floyd and Orville Moody showed up for the sudden-death playoff but were summarily vanquished as Nicklaus buried a birdie on the first extra hole.

The record that appeared most likely to be broken in 1974 was for rainfall. Thursday's round was scrapped after only 20 pros managed to complete 18 holes. Friday proved only slightly better, with two rookies emerging atop the leaderboard. "Who?" replied Nicklaus when asked to comment on co-leaders Barney Thompson and Gary McCord. On Saturday the rain subsided—and gave way to hail. Sunday's third round was halted temporarily but completed eventually. Monday was worse than Sunday,

and Tuesday worse than Monday, at which point Johnny Miller was declared the 54-hole winner.

Miller vs. Nicklaus. The 1975 Crosby had all the buzz of a heavyweight prizefight, especially after Miller had KO'd the field in Phoenix and Tucson, winning both tournaments with a 49-under-par, including a pair of blistering 61s. Alas, the anticipation was greater than the reality as both Nicklaus and Miller hovered on the leaderboard but neither could muster a serious challenge. Youth and notice were served by 25-year-old Stanford grad Tom Watson, who grabbed a share of the second-round lead with birdies on his final four holes at Pebble: Nos. 6, 7, 8, and 9. But Watson shot himself out of contention with a final round 81, and in the end the feel-good story of 1975 was 44-year-old champion Gene Littler.

Kathryn and Bing Crosby with President Gerald Ford

Snoopy graced the cover of the 1976 souvenir program, courtesy of *Peanuts* creator and Clambake regular Charles Schulz. The story, however, remained the same, with good ol' Jack Nicklaus holding the lead heading into Sunday's final round. Channeling his inner Charlie Brown, Nicklaus scuffed his way around Pebble Beach in 82 strokes, including a back nine 45 lowlighted by two triple bogeys. (One writer wondered whether Nicklaus even knew what they called 3-over-par in golf.) After lacing his second shot into the cove along the 18th hole, Nicklaus remarked, "I had driven the ball so darned far that I figured I was going to shoot 79." With no disrespect to worthy champion Ben Crenshaw, that Crosby is still remembered as the one that Jack let get away.

On January 20, 1977, President Gerald Ford

began his day in Washington, D.C., at the inauguration of his successor, Jimmy Carter, and ended it on the driving range at Pebble Beach. Dubbed the world's most famous 15-handicapper, Ford's reputation for hitting the occasional errant shot belied a respectable game for a recreational golfer. Any disappointment at having lost a close election must have been left at the door of the White House, as the former president was all smiles playing with partner Arnold Palmer before a massive gallery.

Tom Watson wowed the crowds with a tournament record score of 14-under-par 273, though it came down to the very last putt. Englishman Tony Jacklin, trailing by one going to No. 18, missed a three-foot par putt that would have forced a playoff. Afterwards, Watson recalled how, as a student just up the road at Stanford, he would leave campus at five o'clock in the morning and barrel down to Pebble Beach, where longtime starter Ray Parga would let him tee off for free before the paying customers arrived.

Due to work in progress at Spyglass Hill, the Crosby returned to the Monterey Peninsula Country Club Shore Course for the first time in a decade. Another notable first that year: women, including LPGA rookie sensation Nancy Lopez, participated in the Clambake for the first time since Babe Didrickson Zaharias played with the boys back in the Rancho Santa Fe days.

The cover of the 1978 program did not feature the usual artist rendering, but rather a handsome photograph of the host, who had died, fittingly, on a golf course near Madrid, Spain, three months earlier. (The 74-year-old Crosby posted an 85 in his last earthly round of golf.) "My mother asked me if I thought we should continue the tournament," recalled Bing's son Nathaniel, who, at age 16, stepped in as the tournament host. "I said, 'Sure, it's what Dad wanted.'"

A storm washed out the first round, the heavy rains seemingly symbolic of tears from on high over the loss of Bing. But true to the old showbiz saw "the show must go on," play resumed and Tom Watson picked up right where he'd left off. He held a share of the lead before Monday's final round, then found himself in the same position afterwards. The playoff ended on the second hole when Ben Crenshaw could not match Watson's par at No. 17. Watson joined Sam Snead, Cary Middlecoff, and Jack Nicklaus as the only back-to-back champions in Crosby history. Watson's bid for a historic three-peat got derailed by a second round 76 at the 1979 Crosby, won in a three-hole playoff by Lon Hinkle.

The year after his passing, Bing Crosby received a richly deserved honor when he was inducted into the World Golf Hall of Fame.

Arnold Palmer, Bob Hope, and Phil Harris
William C. Brooks/Pebble Beach Company Lagorio Archives

1970

JANUARY 22–25

CYPRESS POINT CLUB
PEBBLE BEACH GOLF LINKS
SPYGLASS HILL GOLF COURSE

PROFESSIONALS

Bert Yancey	1	67	70	72	69	278	$25,000
Jack Nicklaus	2	70	72	72	65	279	
Howie Johnson	T3	68	74	71	70	283	
Bobby Nichols	T3	71	73	69	70	283	

PRO-AM TEAMS

Bob Rosburg	1	61	63	64	64	252
John Brodie						
Mason Rudolph	2	64	64	62	63	253
Morgan Barofsky						

Whitman Associates, PROGRAM DESIGN

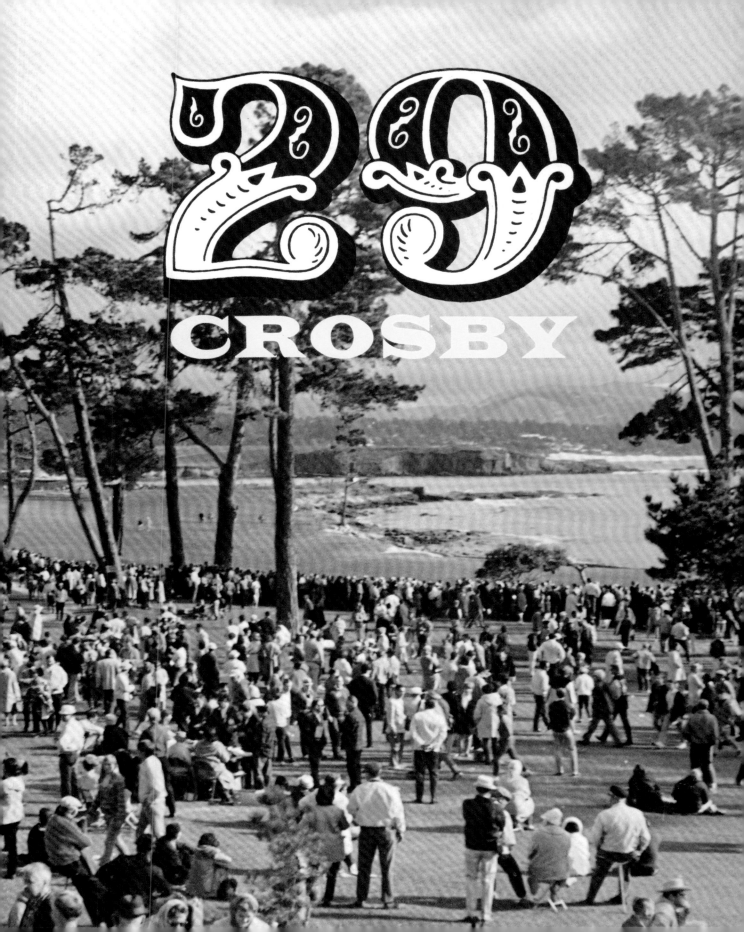

29
CROSBY

1971

JANUARY 14–17

CYPRESS POINT CLUB
PEBBLE BEACH GOLF LINKS
SPYGLASS HILL GOLF COURSE

PROFESSIONALS

Tom Shaw	1	68	71	69	70	278	$27,000
Arnold Palmer	2	72	68	69	71	280	
Bob Murphy	3	71	69	73	69	282	

PRO-AM TEAMS

Lou Graham	1	64	64	61	65	254
Father John Durkin						
Jack Burke Jr.	2	65	60	66	64	255
George Coleman						

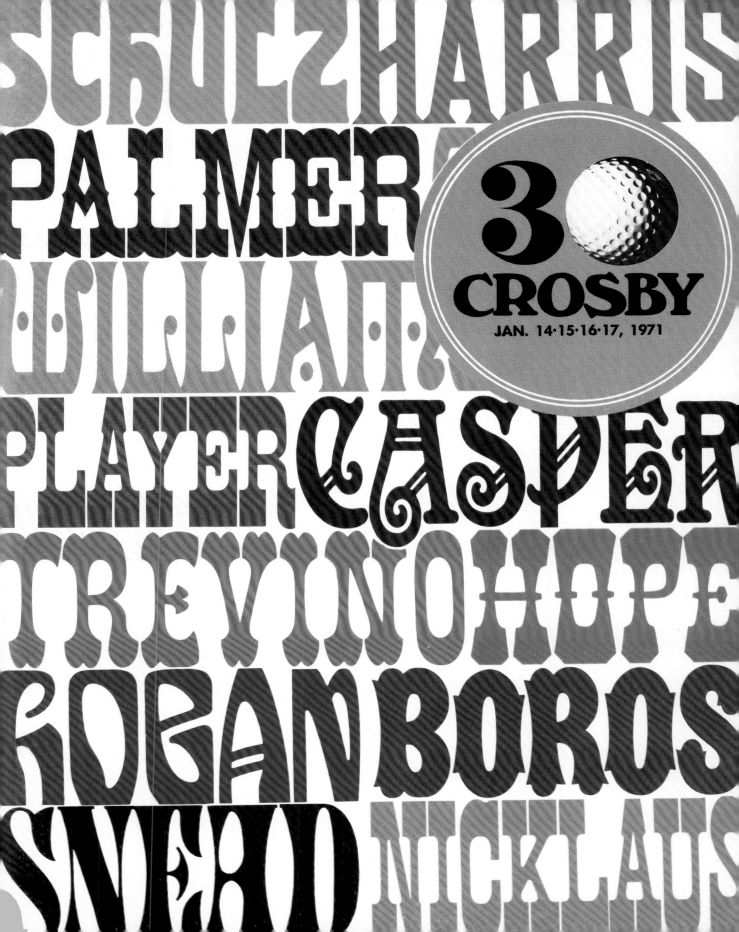

1972

JANUARY 13–16

CYPRESS POINT CLUB
PEBBLE BEACH GOLF LINKS
SPYGLASS HILL GOLF COURSE

PROFESSIONALS

Jack Nicklaus*	1	66	74	71	73	284	$28,000
Johnny Miller	2	75	68	67	74	284	
Lee Trevino	3	69	74	70	73	286	

*playoff

PRO-AM TEAMS

| Lee Trevino
Don Schwab | 1 | 66 | 67 | 59 | 64 | 256 |
| Bob Murphy
Tommy Vickers | 2 | 68 | 67 | 60 | 65 | 260 |

31
Crosby

1973

JANUARY 25–28

CYPRESS POINT CLUB
PEBBLE BEACH GOLF LINKS
SPYGLASS HILL GOLF COURSE

PROFESSIONALS

Jack Nicklaus*	1	71	69	71	71	282	$36,000
Raymond Floyd	T2	71	70	70	71	282	
Orville Moody	T2	71	66	69	76	282	

*playoff

PRO-AM TEAMS

Lanny Wadkins Billy Satterfield	1	64	58	62	71	255
Jim Simmons Garth Reynolds	2	61	68	68	65	262

Al Parker, ARTIST

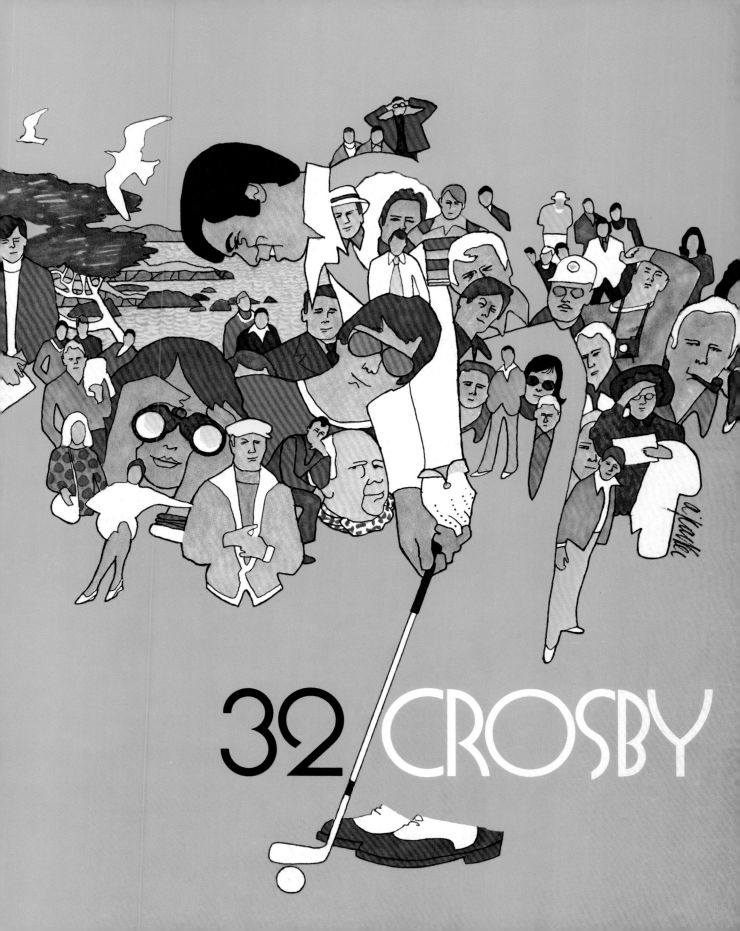

32 CROSBY

1974

JANUARY 3–6

CYPRESS POINT CLUB
PEBBLE BEACH GOLF LINKS
SPYGLASS HILL GOLF COURSE

PROFESSIONALS

Johnny Miller	1	68	70	70	208	$27,500
Grier Jones	2	71	69	72	212	
Rod Funseth	T3	72	70	72	214	
Tom Kite	T3	71	75	68	214	
Bruce Summerhays	T3	74	71	69	214	
John Jacobs	T3	74	68	72	214	

PRO-AM TEAMS

Johnny Miller Locke de Bretteville	1	64	67	65	196
B. R. McLendon David Kirkland	2	67	66	64	197

33 Crosby

1975

JANUARY 23–26

CYPRESS POINT CLUB
PEBBLE BEACH GOLF LINKS
SPYGLASS HILL GOLF COURSE

PROFESSIONALS

Gene Littler	1	68	71	68	73	280	$37,000
Hubert Green	2	66	75	74	69	284	
Tom Kite	3	70	76	69	70	285	

PRO-AM TEAMS

Bruce Devlin Jacky Lee	1	67	63	63	67	260
Tom Watson Robert Willits	T2	64	64	68	67	263
Hubert Green Louis Auer	T2	61	68	67	67	263

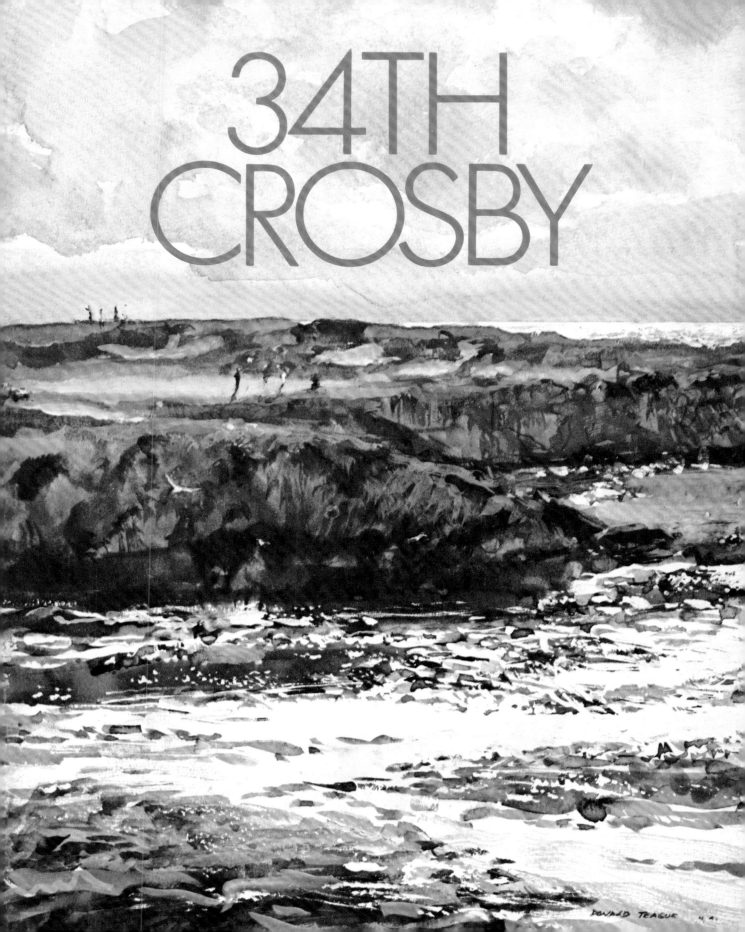

34TH
CROSBY

1976

JANUARY 22–25

CYPRESS POINT CLUB
PEBBLE BEACH GOLF LINKS
SPYGLASS HILL GOLF COURSE

PROFESSIONALS

Ben Crenshaw	1	75	67	70	69	281	$37,000
Mike Morley	2	67	72	71	73	283	
George Burns	T3	74	72	69	69	284	
Dave Hill	T3	71	65	76	72	284	

PRO-AM TEAMS

Hale Irwin	1	72	63	62	66	263
Darius Keaton						
Hubert Green	T2	66	68	67	63	264
Louis Auer						
Johnny Miller	T2	66	69	66	63	264
Dean Wendt						

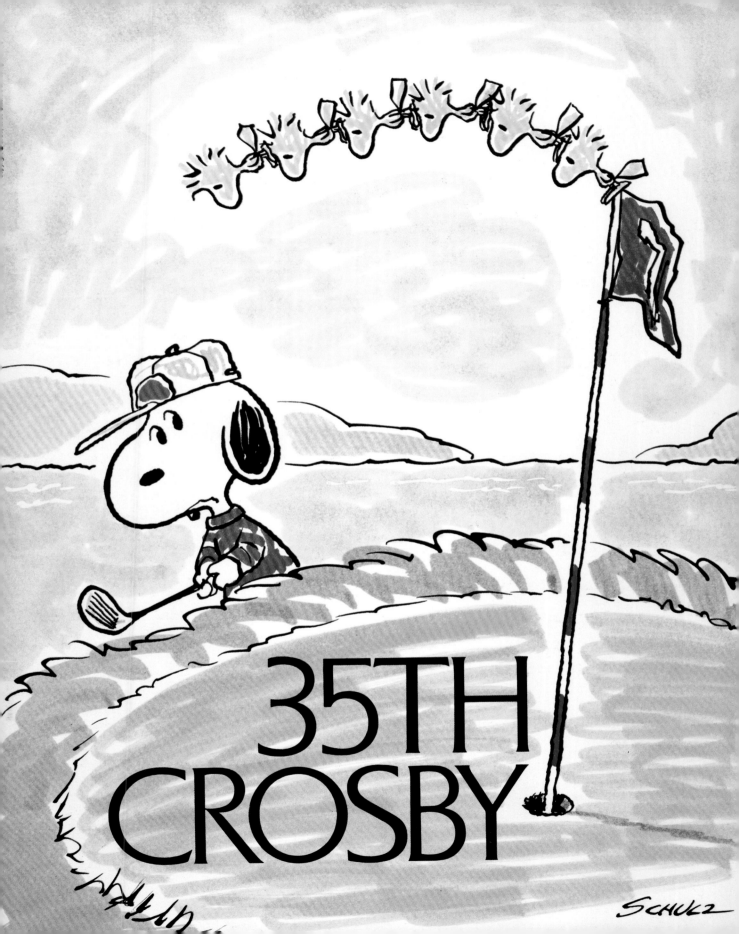

1977

JANUARY 20–23

CYPRESS POINT CLUB
MONTEREY PENINSULA COUNTRY CLUB
PEBBLE BEACH GOLF LINKS

PROFESSIONALS

Tom Watson	1	66	69	67	71	273	$40,000
Tony Jacklin	2	69	66	68	71	274	
Lee Elder	3	69	66	69	71	275	

PRO-AM TEAMS

Leonard Thompson Jim Vickers	1	63	64	64	61	252
Craig Stadler John Jennings	T2	64	62	63	66	255
Hale Irwin Darius Keaton	T2	65	62	62	66	255

Bruce Bomberger, ARTIST

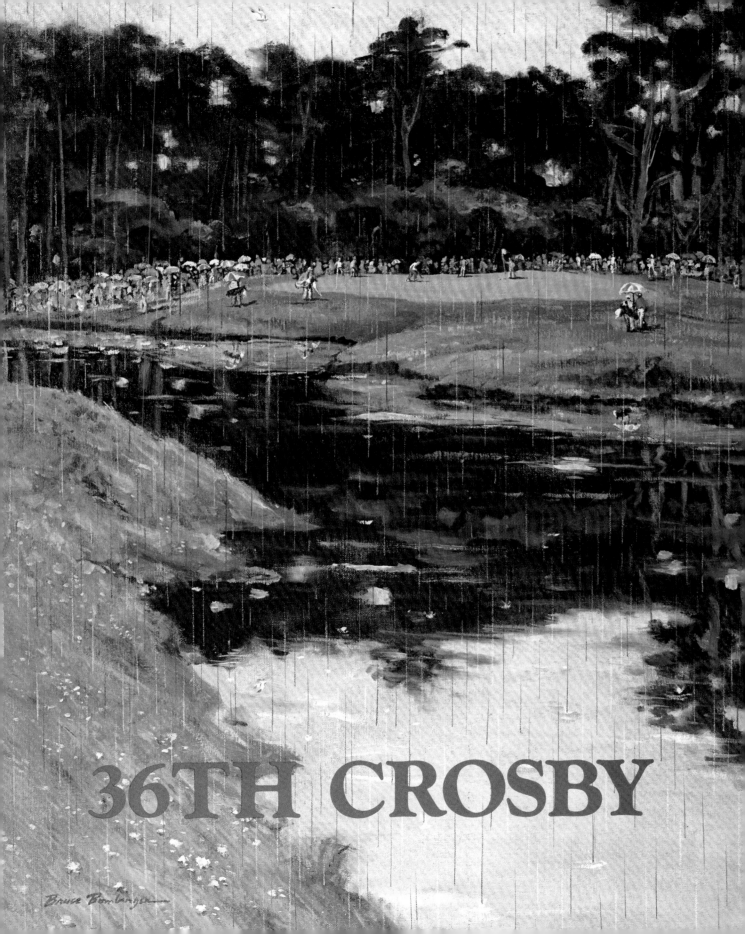

36TH CROSBY

Bruce Bomberger

1978

CYPRESS POINT CLUB
PEBBLE BEACH GOLF LINKS
SPYGLASS HILL GOLF COURSE

PROFESSIONALS

Tom Watson*	1	66	74	71	69	280	$45,000
Ben Crenshaw	2	69	71	73	67	280	
Hale Irwin	3	69	70	74	68	281	

*playoff

PRO-AM TEAMS

Gibby Gilbert Richard Gelb	1	65	63	67	65	260
Tony Jacklin Jim Mahoney	2	67	64	67	63	261

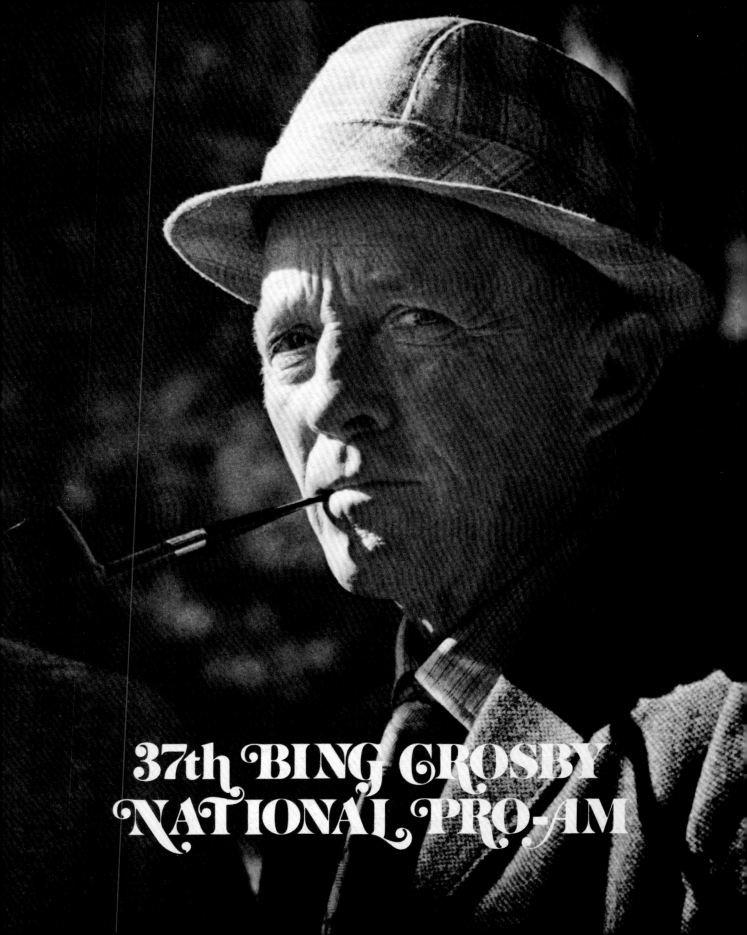

37th BING CROSBY NATIONAL PRO-AM

1979

CYPRESS POINT CLUB
PEBBLE BEACH GOLF LINKS
SPYGLASS HILL GOLF COURSE

PROFESSIONALS

Lon Hinkle*	1	70	68	69	77	284	$54,000
Mark Hayes	T2	73	73	66	72	284	
Andy Bean	T2	72	73	70	69	284	

*playoff

PRO-AM TEAMS

Andy Bean Bill Bunting	1	67	65	61	64	257
Gary Koch Bob Michael	T2	66	66	64	67	263
Lee Trevino Don Schwab	T2	65	66	65	67	263

38th BING CROSBY
NATIONAL PRO-AM

The 1980s

T HE CROSBY BEGAN THE '80S WITH A BANG—LITERALLY—WHEN DEFENDING CHAMP LON HINKLE HAD TO SMASH THE WINDOW OF HIS RENTAL CAR, IN WHICH HE'D LOCKED HIS KEYS, IN ORDER TO GET HIS GOLF CLUBS RIGHT BEFORE THE FIRST ROUND. DAVID EDWARDS, PLAYING IN HIS FIRST CLAMBAKE, ENJOYED A THREE-STROKE EDGE OVER GEORGE BURNS III AND JACK NICKLAUS; HOWEVER, IT WAS NOT NICKLAUS WHO RALLIED BUT RATHER BURNS, ROLLING IN A 45-FOOT BIRDIE PUTT AT NO. 16 THAT VAULTED HIM TO HIS FIRST VICTORY ON TOUR.

Crosby weather continued to dazzle and drench, often in the same week. The first two days were a total wash in 1981, then the sun shined bright for the 54-hole finish. Monday's final round ended with a five-way tie between Carmel native Bobby Clampett, past champion Ben Crenshaw, Barney Thompson, Hale Irwin, and John Cook. On the third extra hole, Cook, a former U.S. and California Amateur champion, was the last man standing, and for the second year in a row the winner made the Crosby his first Tour victory.

Later that summer, Nathaniel Crosby made golfing history of his own when the 19-year-old won the United States Amateur at the Olympic Club in San Francisco. With the sort of dramatic flair for which Bing was better known, the prodigy son birdied the first playoff hole to become the youngest champion in U.S. Amateur history (a record Crosby would later relinquish to Tiger Woods).

The Crosby had always been colorful, but perhaps never more so than in 1982, when first-round leader Bruce Lietzke played Pebble Beach with a chartreuse ball and Jerry Pate made a hole in one at Cypress Point's famous 16th with an orange ball. It was reported to be only the sixth ace ever at the picturesque par-3, with the first coming in 1947 courtesy of Bing. Craig Stadler led the tournament by five strokes with 10 holes to play but sputtered coming in and was passed by eventual champion Jim Simons.

Under skies so ominous that the Goodyear Blimp had to turn around and go home, 1983 final round leader Tom Kite carded bogeys at the 15th, 16th, and 17th holes; his cushion, however,

Mark O'Meara

had been padded the day before at Pebble Beach with a course record 62, an astounding round in which Kite needed but 21 putts.

The following year, a pair of ricochets—one famous, the other infamous—marked the 1984 Crosby. Living up to his reputation for erratic ball striking, former President Gerald Ford clocked a lady on the noggin at Spyglass Hill on Friday. On Sunday Hale Irwin came to No. 18 one stroke behind Jim Nelford, but his hopes were dashed when his drive sailed left and into the rocks—only to bound back into the fairway. Irwin made a birdie to force a playoff and then another to end it following a spectacular approach from a fairway bunker at No. 16.

Whipping winds sent scores soaring in 1985, with only nine players shooting under par in the first round. Johnny Miller held the lead into the weekend, but Sunday dawned with Mark O'Meara atop the leaderboard. After making clutch pars at Nos. 17 and 18 to preserve his one-stroke lead, O'Meara had to stand aside and watch. When Curtis Strange's 13-foot birdie putt failed to fall, O'Meara had claimed the crown in what would be the final Crosby Clambake.

The AT&T Pebble Beach National Pro-Am debuted in 1986. The new tournament sponsor ensured that the legacy of the Crosby Clambake would live on, rain or shine. That year it rained. The first round was delayed but ultimately played. Friday's second round was cancelled, as was Monday's final round, and 54-hole leader Fuzzy Zoeller was declared the winner over runner-up Payne Stewart. Stewart came up short again the following year, finishing second again in 1987 after failing to hold a five-stroke lead. A flurry of birdies saw Johnny Miller climb onto and all the way up the leaderboard on the way to his second tournament championship.

Baseball Hall of Famer George Brett claimed the team title with pro partner Fred Couples in 1987, then Football Hall of Famer Dan Marino

Tom Watson

took the honors with Dan Pohl in 1988. Greg Norman made a Sunday charge that year with a 66 but finished one stroke shy of the playoff between Steve Jones and Bob Tway. After a bogey at No. 17 dropped Jones into a tie with Tway during regulation, a birdie at the same hole in sudden death added Jones to the list of pros that made this tournament their first PGA Tour victory.

In 1989 a couple of good old boys got in on the action early: Dave Stockton, age 47, claimed the first-round lead, and Jack Nicklaus, 49, took a turn on the weekend leaderboard before a third-round 80 knocked him out of contention. There would be no first-time winner this time, as the duel came down to a pair of past champions. Tom Kite carded a final round 69—one stroke better than Mark O'Meara on the day, but one stroke shy for the tournament, giving O'Meara his fourth career victory and his second at Pebble Beach. It would not be his last.

1980

JANUARY 31–FEBRUARY 3

CYPRESS POINT CLUB
PEBBLE BEACH GOLF LINKS
SPYGLASS HILL GOLF COURSE

PROFESSIONALS

George Burns	1	71	69	71	69	280	$54,000
Dan Pohl	2	72	70	72	67	281	
John Mahaffey	T3	68	74	72	68	282	
Keith Fergus	T3	70	71	71	70	282	
Bill Kratzert	T3	70	74	68	70	282	
Larry Nelson	T3	70	70	70	72	282	

PRO-AM TEAMS

| George Cadle Wheeler Farish | T1 | 62 | 65 | 66 | 65 | 258 |
| John Mahaffey Vern Peak | T1 | 66 | 65 | 64 | 63 | 258 |

Al Parker, ARTIST

89/CROSBY

1981

JANUARY 29–FEBRUARY 1

CYPRESS POINT CLUB
PEBBLE BEACH GOLF LINKS
SPYGLASS HILL GOLF COURSE

PROFESSIONALS

John Cook*	1	66	71	72	209	$40,500
Hale Irwin	T2	70	69	70	209	
Barney Thompson	T2	71	71	67	209	
Bobby Clampett	T2	67	71	71	209	
Ben Crenshaw	T2	67	70	72	209	

*playoff

PRO-AM TEAMS

George Cadle Wheeler Farish	1	65	62	64	191
Tom Kite Tom Kite Sr.	2	63	67	64	194

Eldon Dedini, ARTIST

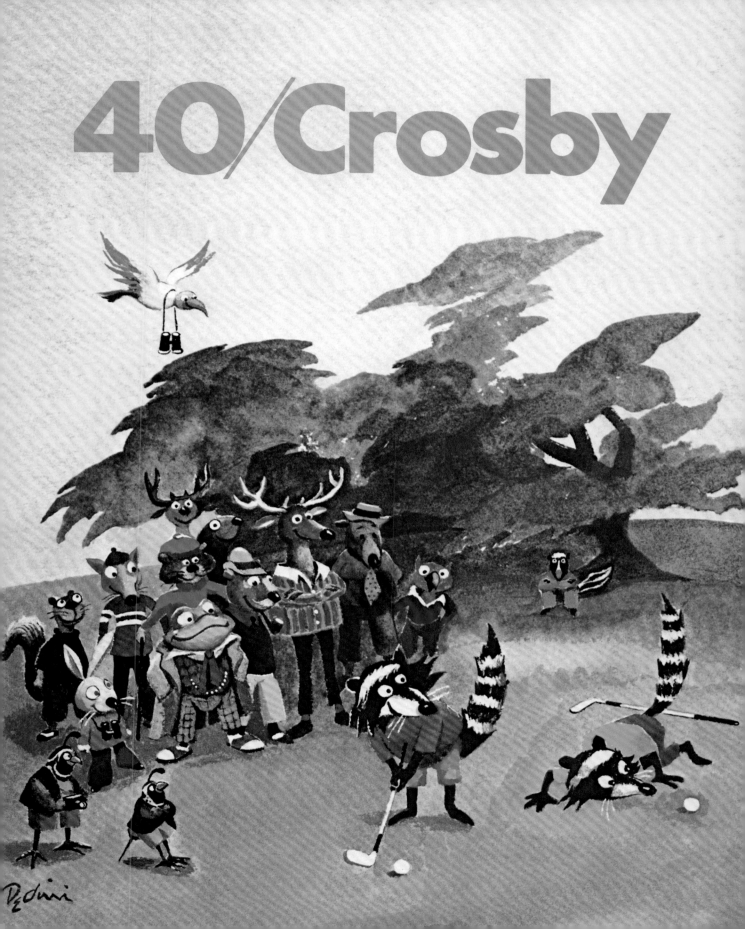

40/Crosby

1982

FEBRUARY 4–7

CYPRESS POINT CLUB
PEBBLE BEACH GOLF LINKS
SPYGLASS HILL GOLF COURSE

PROFESSIONALS

Jim Simons	1	71	66	71	66	274	$54,000
Craig Stadler	2	71	71	64	70	276	
Johnny Miller	T3	71	71	71	67	280	
Mike Morley	T3	72	76	65	67	280	
Rex Caldwell	T3	73	67	73	67	280	
Joe Inman	T3	73	69	69	69	280	
Jack Nicklaus	T3	69	70	71	70	280	

PRO-AM TEAMS

Jay Haas Alfonso Fanjul	1	68	64	63	62	257
Gibby Gilbert Richard Gelb	2	65	60	68	65	258

1983

FEBRUARY 3–6

CYPRESS POINT CLUB
PEBBLE BEACH GOLF LINKS
SPYGLASS HILL GOLF COURSE

PROFESSIONALS

Tom Kite	1	69	72	62	73	276	$58,500
Rex Caldwell	T2	69	70	66	73	278	
Calvin Peete	T2	68	70	70	70	278	

PRO-AM TEAMS

Bob Gilder	1	63	64	65	66	258
Howard Clark						
Victor Regalado	2	62	61	67	70	260
Andres Kaneda						

Donald Teague, N.A., ARTIST

42ND CROSBY

DONALD TEAGUE N.A.

1984

FEBRUARY 2–5

CYPRESS POINT CLUB
PEBBLE BEACH GOLF LINKS
SPYGLASS HILL GOLF COURSE

PROFESSIONALS

Hale Irwin*	1	69	69	68	72	278	$72,000
Jim Nelford	2	67	73	70	68	278	
Mark O'Meara	T3	68	74	68	70	280	
Fred Couples	T3	74	67	69	70	280	

*playoff

PRO-AM TEAMS

| Mark O'Meara J. P. Diesel | 1 | 62 | 67 | 67 | 61 | 257 |
| Rex Caldwell Barry Ruhl | 2 | 66 | 63 | 66 | 63 | 258 |

© LeRoy Neiman, Inc., ARTIST

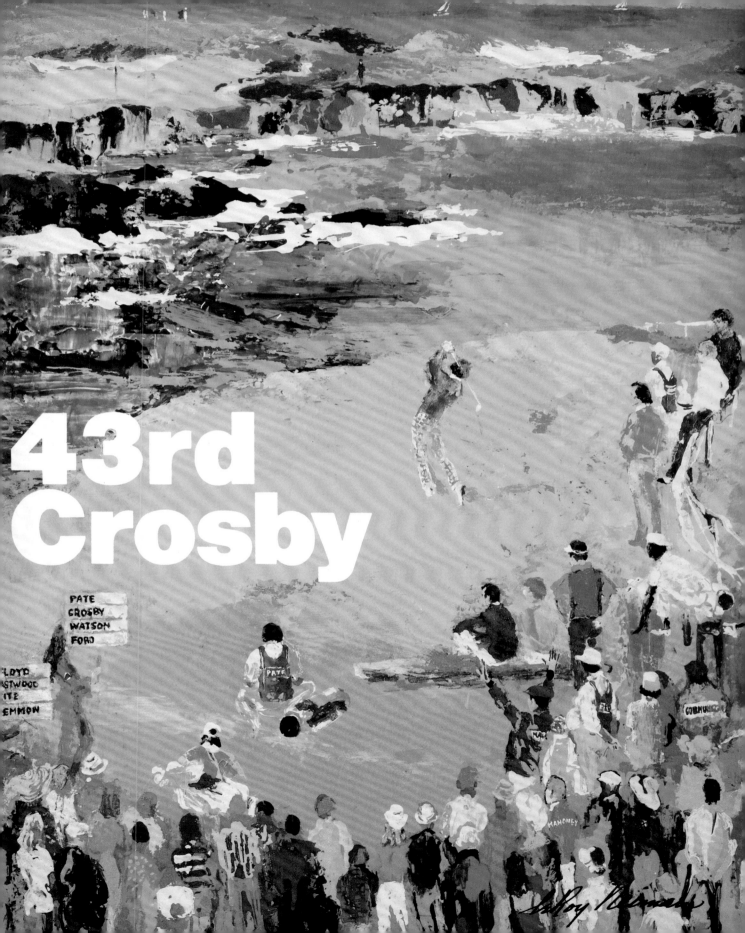

1985

JANUARY 31–FEBRUARY 3

CYPRESS POINT CLUB
PEBBLE BEACH GOLF LINKS
SPYGLASS HILL GOLF COURSE

PROFESSIONALS

Mark O'Meara	1	70	72	68	73	283	$90,000
Kikuo Arai	T2	73	69	71	71	284	
Larry Rinker	T2	73	72	70	69	284	
Curtis Strange	T2	75	69	68	72	284	

PRO-AM TEAMS

Hubert Green Dean Spanos	1	65	63	61	66	255
Jack Nicklaus Jack Nicklaus Jr.	T2	69	65	65	65	264
Dave Eichelberger Pard Erdman	T2	66	66	69	63	264

Thom Thomas, ARTIST

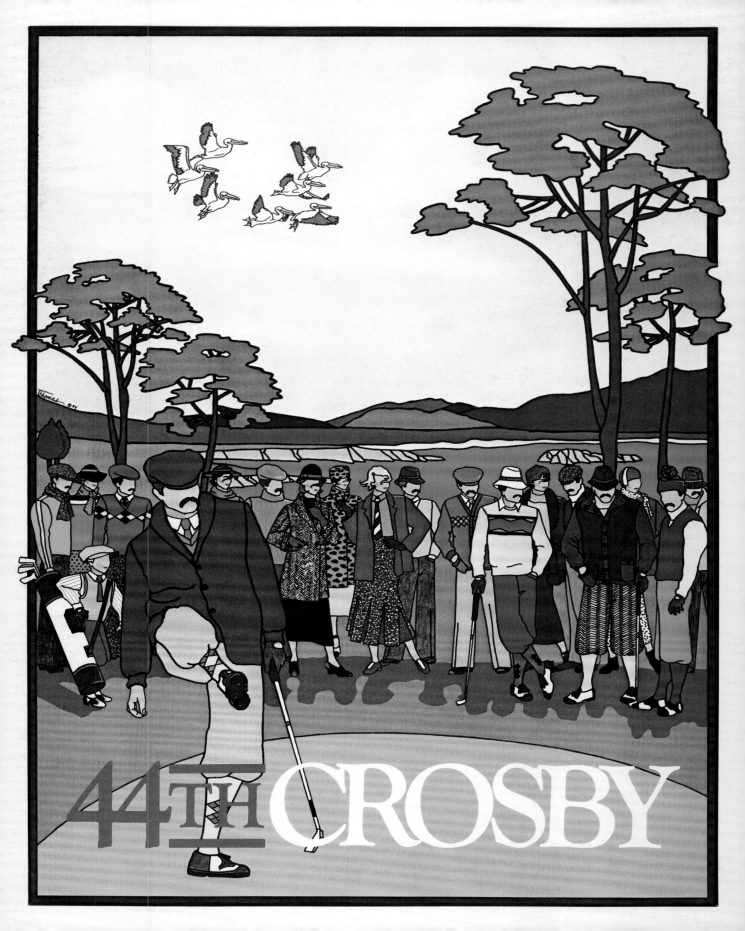

1986

JANUARY 30–FEBRUARY 2

CYPRESS POINT CLUB
PEBBLE BEACH GOLF LINKS
SPYGLASS HILL GOLF COURSE

PROFESSIONALS

Fuzzy Zoeller	1	69	66	70	205	$108,000
Payne Stewart	2	71	69	70	210	
Mark Wiebe	T3	70	69	72	211	
Tom Watson	T3	71	67	73	211	
Tony Sills	T3	72	68	71	211	

PRO-AM TEAMS

Fuzzy Zoeller Mike Evans	1	66	62	65	193
Lee Trevino Don Schwab	2	70	68	59	197

1987

JANUARY 29–FEBRUARY 1

CYPRESS POINT CLUB
PEBBLE BEACH GOLF LINKS
SPYGLASS HILL GOLF COURSE

PROFESSIONALS

Johnny Miller	1	72	72	68	66	278	$108,000
Payne Stewart	2	69	69	69	72	279	
Bernhard Langer	T3	72	69	68	71	280	
Lanny Wadkins	T3	68	69	72	71	280	

PRO-AM TEAMS

Fred Couples	1	67	61	64	64	256*
George Brett						
Wayne Levi	2	63	62	68	63	256
Jacky Lee						

*playoff

© LeRoy Neiman, Inc., ARTIST

AT&T
Pebble Beach
National
Pro-Am

1988

CYPRESS POINT CLUB
PEBBLE BEACH GOLF LINKS
SPYGLASS HILL GOLF COURSE

PROFESSIONALS

Steve Jones*	1	72	64	70	74	280	$126,000
Bob Tway	2	72	73	67	68	280	
Greg Norman	3	68	75	72	66	281	

*playoff

PRO-AM TEAMS

Dan Pohl Dan Marino	1	64	63	64	64	255
Steve Jones James Rheim	T2	64	62	67	64	257
Johnny Miller John Miller Jr.	T2	64	62	67	64	257

Edwin Adamson, ARTIST

AT&T PEBBLE BEACH NATIONAL PRO-AM

EDWIN ADAMSON

1989

JANUARY 26–29

CYPRESS POINT CLUB
PEBBLE BEACH GOLF LINKS
SPYGLASS HILL GOLF COURSE

PROFESSIONALS

Mark O'Meara	1	66	68	73	70	277	$180,000
Tom Kite	2	67	70	72	69	278	
Jim Carter	T3	70	72	69	69	280	
Nick Price	T3	66	74	67	73	280	
Sandy Lyle	T3	68	72	72	68	280	

PRO-AM TEAMS

| Steve Jones James Rheim | 1 | 64 | 64 | 63 | 64 | 255 |
| Dan Pohl Dan Marino | 2 | 64 | 65 | 64 | 63 | 256 |

The 1990s

History repeated itself as Mark O'Meara went back to back to win the AT&T Pebble Beach National Pro-Am in 1990, although this win was made all the more special because O'Meara achieved it with his 61-year-old father, Bob, as his amateur playing partner. Brutal winds tested the pros' talent—and patience. Ed Dougherty had a hard time marking his ball and 11-putted the 17th hole at Cypress Point. Bob Gilder, who was tied for the third round lead when he teed off at Cypress Point on Saturday, shot 85 and got blown clear out of the tournament; it was the first time anyone could remember a third-round leader missing the cut. Tom Kite, Payne Stewart, and Rocco Mediate all had their chances, but none could capitalize, not against what had become a distinct home-course advantage for three-time champion O'Meara.

Poppy Hills joined the rotation for the first time in 1991, replacing Cypress Point. Designed by Robert Trent Jones Jr. and opened in 1986, the home course of the Northern California Golf Association proved to be a fair challenge. Paul Azinger was glum after failing to match par in his first crack at the course, but his mood brightened considerably along with the weather on Sunday, as he rode a final round 67 to a four-shot win over Corey Pavin and Brian Claar.

After missing the cut in 1991 and giving someone else a turn to lift the trophy, Mark O'Meara reclaimed his throne the following year. O'Meara hardly registered on the rearview mirror of frontrunner Jeff Sluman, who enjoyed a comfortable four-stroke advantage at the turn on a gorgeous Sunday when birdies were there for the taking. Improbably, though not unexpectedly given his record, O'Meara made a long birdie putt from the fringe on the final hole. Sluman matched him there, but despite having a shorter putt on the first playoff hole, he could not get the best of O'Meara, who took top honors for the third time in four years and joined Sam Snead as the event's only four-time champions.

Payne Stewart

Bill Murray

The year 1992 saw the debut of Bill Murray, who was paired that first year with pro John Adams. Murray's antics, including donning a cap shaped like the Hubert H. Humphrey Metrodome and downing a Polish sausage and a beer on the first tee at Spyglass Hill, made him an instant fan favorite. Not everyone appreciated his unique brand of golf humor, and there was talk that he might not be invited back. But 1987 U.S. Open champion Scott Simpson, a quiet sort who seemed the most unlikely match for Murray, requested the comic as his partner in 1993 and was rewarded with a front-row seat for many of the tournament's most hilariously memorable moments.

In his first time playing the tournament, Australian Brett Ogle not only won his first Tour event, he also became just the second foreign-born golfer to win the National Pro-Am. Ogle was a pleasant surprise but nothing compared to the shocker of 1994 when two lions of the winter roared back to recapture bygone glory. Tom Watson, age 44 and six-plus years removed from

the winner's circle, said he played well enough to win but admitted he did not putt well enough; holding a one-shot lead on the 16th hole, Watson 3-putted that green and the next. Johnny Miller, 46 years old and of fragile knees and unpredictable putter, shot a final-round 74, which was just enough to nose out Watson, Jeff Maggert, Corey Pavin, and Kirk Triplett. It was Miller's first victory since winning the same event seven years earlier and also the last of his illustrious career. It also earned Miller the distinction of being the only golfer to win the event in three different decades.

Another sage pro kept the young guns at bay in 1995. Coming off a missed cut and five-year winless drought, expectations were as low for 40-year-old Peter Jacobsen as they were high for rookie phenom David Duval, a four-time first-team All-American and collegiate National Player of the Year in his first full year on Tour. Following an open round 72, Duval fired three consecutive 67s for

Chris Lemmon and Jack Lemmon

a total of 273. Jacobsen's 65 on Sunday gave him the title by two but, alas, his superlative score in the pro portion was, alone, not enough to carry Jack Lemmon to the promised land on Sunday. Playing Poppy Hills on Saturday, Jacobsen made double bogey on the par-5 final hole, leaving it up to Lemmon: Make par and make the cut. But hard-luck Lemmon carded a quadruple-bogey 9 and missed again.

Never in the history of the tournament, and not since 1949 on the PGA Tour, had an event been cancelled, but El Niño pounded the Monterey Peninsula with such vengeance in 1996 that golfers simply could not get in more than 36 holes. That year will forever be remembered for what could have been, as an epic battle appeared at hand between second-round leader Jeff Maggert and a cadre of challengers featuring past champions Davis Love III, Steve Jones, and Tom Watson.

A phenomenon unlike anything anyone had

seen before descended upon the tournament in 1997: Tiger Woods. His first appearance in the AT&T Pro-Am got off to a slow start. Perhaps it was the unique format or the distractions caused by his high-profile pairing with movie star Kevin Costner, but after two rounds Woods stood ten strokes back of leader Jim Furyk. In what would soon become a familiar scene on the PGA Tour, Woods vaulted into contention with a 63 on Saturday, though David Duval did him one better. His course-record-tying 62 at Pebble Beach gave Duval a three-stroke lead come Sunday over Furyk and—surprise, surprise—Mark O'Meara, while Woods was seven back. Duval's final round 71 tied him with Woods, who finished birdie-birdie-birdie to shoot 64, but the past prevailed over the future when O'Meara posted a fourth consecutive 67 to claim an unprecedented fifth title.

In 1998 El Niño rains cut Thursday's and Friday's rounds short at nine holes both days.

Golfers got in 18 holes Saturday, then Sunday and Monday were both wash outs. Determined not to cancel the tournament for the second time in three years, the PGA Tour came up with the novel idea of postponing the event and resuming the final round six months later. Following the finish of the PGA Championship in August, a chartered flight brought a plane filled with tour pros back to Pebble Beach. Not all of the contestants were able to make it, but 125 did, and 198 days later Phil Mickelson won the longest tournament in PGA Tour history by a stroke over Tom Pernice Jr.

Back in January, Jack Lemmon's long wait appeared to finally be over, as he and Peter Jacobsen were safely on the right side of the cut. But in a cruel twist of ill fate, officials battling El Niño and dealing with waterlogged conditions decided to try to preserve the putting greens for the pros by canceling the amateur competition. Lemmon would return and valiantly try once more, but in his final appearance he and Jacobsen missed the cut by three strokes. Jack Lemmon passed away in the summer of 2001.

Payne Stewart must have felt like the Jack Lemmon of the professional ranks, having come close in this tournament so many times, including six top-10s and two runner-up finishes. In 1999 Stewart claimed the 54-hole lead after sinking a tap-in birdie on the 18th hole at Spyglass Hill—though all eyes that week were on the new 5th hole at Pebble Beach. The beachfront par-3 took its rightful place on the plot initially intended for the hole in 1916, after decades of being located inland when the owners of the beachfront land demanded a king's ransom to sell. When the last owner died in 1995, the Pebble Beach Company bought the land and hired Jack Nicklaus to design the hole, which garnered rave reviews and finally fulfilled the original vision.

Incessant rains caused the suspension of play on Sunday morning, and when the weather

Jack Nicklaus

went from bad to worse, the final round was cancelled and Stewart declared the 1999 winner. "I see coming to Pebble Beach as a symbol of my rebirth," Stewart said in an interview not long after his stirring victory later that summer in the U.S. Open at Pinehurst. "To wear the champion's crown there will mean more to me than just simply as a golfer." A few months later, Stewart died tragically in a plane crash. The loss was profound; thankfully, the people's champion left us with the lasting image of a man playing golf, having fun, and beaming an irrepressible smile.

1990

FEBRUARY 1–4

CYPRESS POINT CLUB
PEBBLE BEACH GOLF LINKS
SPYGLASS HILL GOLF COURSE

PROFESSIONALS

Mark O'Meara	1	67	73	69	72	281	$180,000
Kenny Perry	2	73	71	69	70	283	
Tom Kite	T3	69	69	75	71	284	
Payne Stewart	T3	66	71	74	73	284	

PRO-AM TEAMS

Hubert Green Dean Spanos	1	63	68	61	68	260
David Frost Tom Crow	T2	69	63	67	65	264
Bob Eastwood David Fisher	T2	67	65	69	63	264
Mark Calcavecchia Gary Carter	T2	64	67	67	66	264

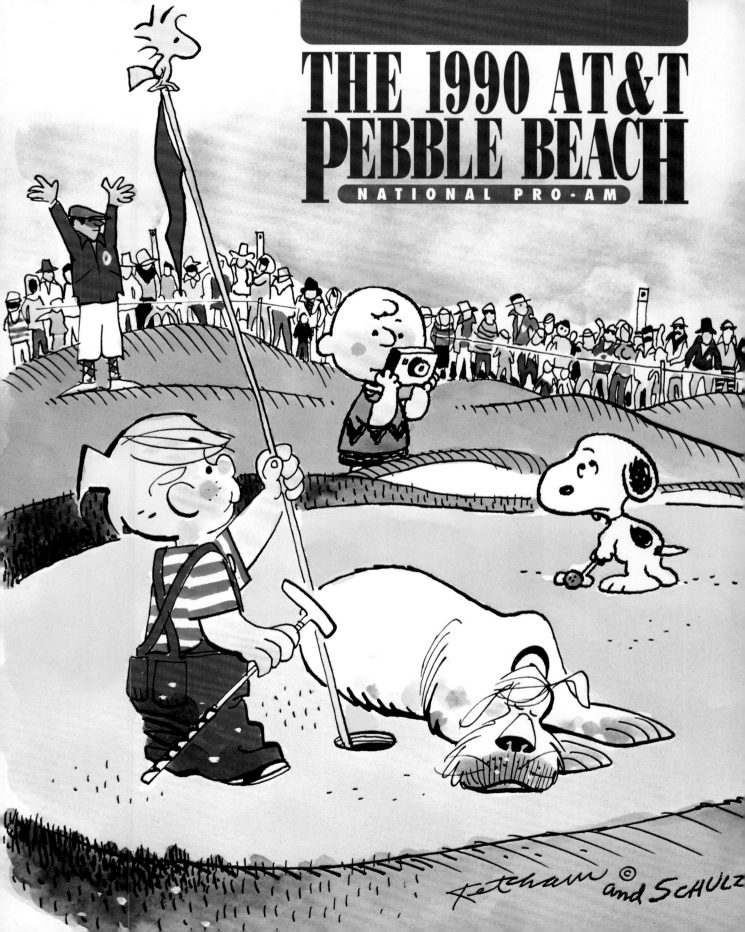

1991

JANUARY 31–FEBRUARY 3

PEBBLE BEACH GOLF LINKS
POPPY HILLS GOLF COURSE
SPYGLASS HILL GOLF COURSE

PROFESSIONALS

Paul Azinger	1	67	67	73	67	274	$198,000
Brian Claar	T2	66	73	71	68	278	
Corey Pavin	T2	71	71	69	67	278	

PRO-AM TEAMS

John Cook	1	63	67	63	62	255
Jack Wagner						
Bobby Wadkins	2	64	64	66	62	256
Vinnie Giles						

THE 1991

AT & T PEBBLE BEACH

NATIONAL PRO-AM

PEBBLE BEACH, CALIFORNIA
JANUARY 31 - FEBRUARY 3, 1991
PEBBLE BEACH ■ POPPY HILLS ■ SPYGLASS HILL

1992

JANUARY 30–FEBRUARY 2

PEBBLE BEACH GOLF LINKS
POPPY HILLS GOLF COURSE
SPYGLASS HILL GOLF COURSE

PROFESSIONALS

Mark O'Meara*	1	69	68	68	70	275	$198,000
Jeff Sluman	2	64	73	70	68	275	
Paul Azinger	3	74	70	64	68	276	

*playoff

PRO-AM TEAMS

Greg Norman	1	63	59	59	65	246
Kerry Packer						
Frank Funk	2	62	66	62	62	252
Lawrence Taylor						

THE 1992

AT&T
PEBBLE
BEACH

NATIONAL PRO-AM

PEBBLE BEACH, CALIFORNIA
JANUARY 30 - FEBRUARY 2, 1992
POPPY HILLS ■ PEBBLE BEACH ■ SPYGLASS HILL

LeRoy Neiman

1993

PEBBLE BEACH GOLF LINKS
POPPY HILLS GOLF COURSE
SPYGLASS HILL GOLF COURSE

PROFESSIONALS

Brett Ogle	1	68	68	69	71	276	$225,000
Billy Ray Brown	2	70	68	69	72	279	
Greg Twiggs	T3	69	72	70	69	280	
Joey Sindelar	T3	69	72	70	69	280	
Trevor Dodds	T3	70	68	70	72	280	

PRO-AM TEAMS

Payne Stewart Jim Morris	1	63	65	63	66	257
Perry Moss Ken Bowden	T2	62	65	64	67	258
Billy Andrade Mark McGwire	T2	65	66	63	64	258
David Edwards Mark Grace	T2	65	66	63	64	258
Willie Wood John Zoller	T2	66	70	60	62	258

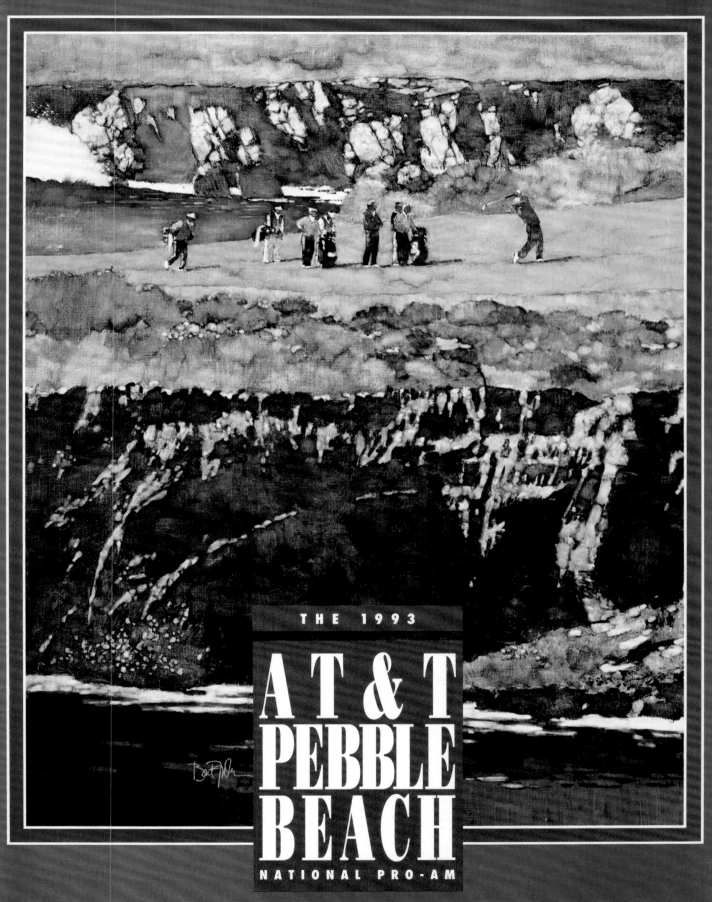

THE 1993

AT & T
PEBBLE
BEACH

NATIONAL PRO-AM

PEBBLE BEACH, CALIFORNIA ■ FEBRUARY 4-7, 1993 ■ POPPY HILLS ■ PEBBLE BEACH ■ SPYGLASS HILL

1994

FEBRUARY 3–6

PEBBLE BEACH GOLF LINKS
POPPY HILLS GOLF COURSE
SPYGLASS HILL GOLF COURSE

PROFESSIONALS

Johnny Miller	1	68	72	67	74	281	$225,000
Jeff Maggert	T2	68	72	72	70	282	
Corey Pavin	T2	69	71	71	71	282	
Kirk Triplett	T2	69	74	67	72	282	
Tom Watson	T2	69	67	72	74	282	

PRO-AM TEAMS

Dudley Hart Robert Floyd	1	58	66	64	70	258
Jim Nelford Robert McDonnell	T2	59	68	66	68	261
Tom Kite Rudy Gatlin	T2	61	64	67	69	261

THE 1994
AT&T PEBBLE BEACH
NATIONAL PRO-AM

PEBBLE BEACH, CALIFORNIA ■ FEBRUARY 3-6, 1994 ■ POPPY HILLS ■ PEBBLE BEACH ■ SPYGLASS HILL

1995

FEBRUARY 2–5

PEBBLE BEACH GOLF LINKS
POPPY HILLS GOLF COURSE
SPYGLASS HILL GOLF COURSE

PROFESSIONALS

Peter Jacobsen	1	67	73	66	65	271	$252,000
David Duval	2	72	67	67	67	273	
Kenny Perry	T3	68	68	67	72	275	
Davis Love III	T3	65	71	71	68	275	

PRO-AM TEAMS

David Duval Hughes Norton	1	69	60	61	64	254
Jack Nicklaus Steve Nicklaus	2	67	63	61	64	255

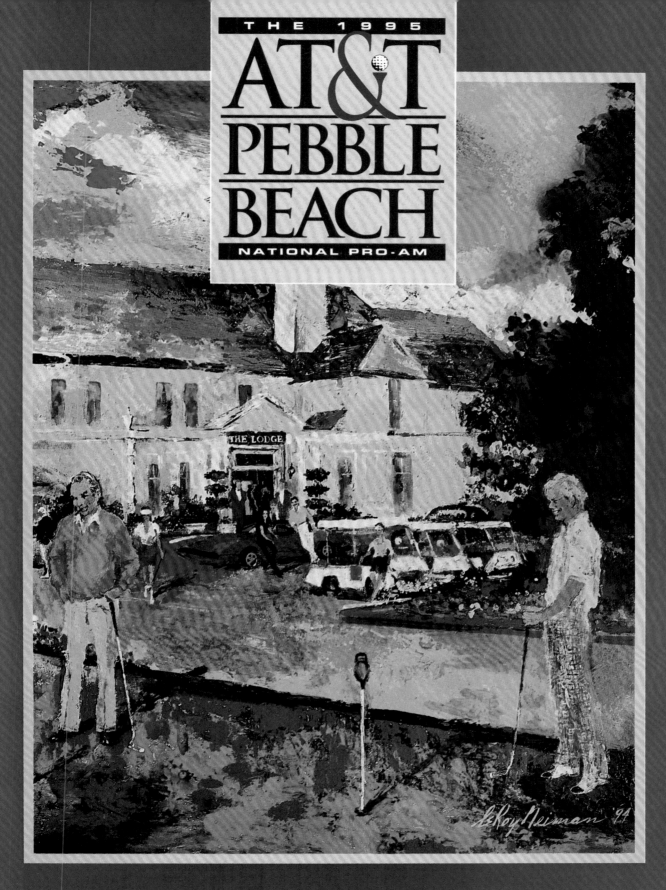

THE 1995
AT&T
PEBBLE
BEACH
NATIONAL PRO·AM

PEBBLE BEACH, CALIFORNIA • FEBRUARY 2-5, 1995 • PEBBLE BEACH • POPPY HILLS • SPYGLASS HILL

1996

FEBRUARY 1–4

PEBBLE BEACH GOLF LINKS
POPPY HILLS GOLF COURSE
SPYGLASS HILL GOLF COURSE

Tournament cancelled due to El Niño

PEBBLE BEACH, CALIFORNIA • FEBRUARY 1-4, 1996 • PEBBLE BEACH • POPPY HILLS • SPYGLASS HILL

1997

JANUARY 30–FEBRUARY 2

PEBBLE BEACH GOLF LINKS
POPPY HILLS GOLF COURSE
SPYGLASS HILL GOLF COURSE

PROFESSIONALS

Mark O'Meara	1	67	67	67	67	268	$342,200
David Duval	T2	65	71	62	71	269	
Tiger Woods	T2	70	72	63	64	269	

PRO-AM TEAMS

Paul Stankowski Andy Garcia	1	62	58	67	58	245
Frank Lickliter Joe Mayernik	T2	60	65	58	65	248
Glen Day Paul Hazen	T2	62	63	62	61	248
Grant Waite Stan Humphries	T2	65	62	63	58	248

John Hargrove ARTIST

THE 1997

AT&T

PEBBLE

BEACH

NATIONAL PRO-AM

HARDGROVE

PEBBLE BEACH, CALIFORNIA • JAN. 30 – FEB. 2, 1997 • PEBBLE BEACH • POPPY HILLS • SPYGLASS HILL

1998

JANUARY 29–FEBRUARY 1

PEBBLE BEACH GOLF LINKS
POPPY HILLS GOLF COURSE
SPYGLASS HILL GOLF COURSE

PROFESSIONALS

Phil Mickelson	1	65	70	67	202	$450,000
Tom Pernice, Jr.	2	67	69	67	203	
Jim Furyk	T3	69	67	68	204	
Paul Azinger	T3	67	69	68	204	
J. P. Hayes	T3	70	67	67	204	

Final round completed on August 17
Pro-Am cancelled

THE 1998
AT&T
PEBBLE
BEACH
NATIONAL PRO-AM

PEBBLE BEACH, CALIFORNIA • JAN. 29 – FEB. 1, 1998 • PEBBLE BEACH • POPPY HILLS • SPYGLASS HILL

1999

FEBRUARY 4–7

PEBBLE BEACH GOLF LINKS
POPPY HILLS GOLF COURSE
SPYGLASS HILL GOLF COURSE

PROFESSIONALS

Payne Stewart	1	69	64	73	206	$504,000
Frank Lickliter	2	68	68	71	207	
Craig Stadler	3	70	67	72	209	

PRO-AM TEAMS

Frank Lickliter Robert MacDonnell	T1	63	65	66	194
Craig Stadler Glenn Frey	T1	65	60	69	194
Neal Lancaster Robert Scott	T1	68	66	60	194

THE 1999

AT&T PEBBLE BEACH

NATIONAL PRO-AM

PEBBLE BEACH, CALIFORNIA • FEBRUARY 4 - 7, 1999 • PEBBLE BEACH • POPPY HILLS • SPYGLASS HILL

The 2000s

Since its inception as the Crosby Clambake, the AT&T Pebble Beach National Pro-Am has more than delivered on Bing's promise of an exciting finish, perhaps never more so than in 2000. Matt Gogel, a six-time winner on the Nike Tour and 29-year-old PGA Tour rookie, was cruising to his first title, but then a funny thing happened on the way to the trophy ceremony. Heading to the 12th tee, seven strokes and five golfers separated Tiger Woods from the top of the leaderboard. Missed birdie putts at Nos. 12 and 14 steamed Woods, who kept his cool while Gogel had a harder time letting go of bogeys at the 11th and 12th holes, especially after his stellar front nine 31. Ahead at the 15th, Woods hit a wedge from 97 yards out to four feet, only to see his ball roll back into the cup for an eagle. Woods almost did it again at the 16th but settled for a tap-in birdie. Another birdie at the home hole established Woods as the clubhouse leader at 15 under par.

Gogel got a look at the leaderboard when he reached No. 16. "To see Tiger's name, well, I was amazed," he said after posting a back nine 40. "I will not be amazed anymore." Gogel had a 10-footer to force a playoff but missed that—and the comebacker, a gaffe that cost him $80,000. Woods's score of 64 was the best finish by a winner in tournament history and his sixth Tour victory in a row.

No less impressive was Davis Love III's Sunday assault on Pebble Beach in 2001. Matt Gogel looked ready to exact some revenge when he broke the Poppy Hills course record with a 10-under-par 62 on Friday, good for a three-shot lead heading into the weekend, but a gaudy 81 on Saturday ended his quest. Love was mired in a tie for fourteenth after Saturday's round, but he made the most of a gloriously sunny Sunday to blister the front nine in a tournament record 28, including an 8-under-par stretch over the first seven holes. "I didn't think I had a chance to win," Love admitted, "yet I recalled Tiger was seven behind with seven holes to play last year and won, so you never know." A steady

1-under-par 35 on the back nine gave Love a final round score of 63. Love had to wait and watch as Phil Mickelson made a charge with birdies at the 16th and 17th holes but, needing birdie at 18, Mickelson decided to hit driver from the fairway and deposited his approach into Stillwater Cove. With that, Love earned his first Tour win in almost three years.

Nothing if not dogged, Matt Gogel aimed to take care of unfinished business in 2002. He got a little help from fiery Pat Perez, whose four-shot final round lead went up in smoke thanks to hitting his approach out of bounds at the par-5 14th hole. Birdies by Perez at Nos. 15 and 17, combined with Gogel's bogey at the 17th, gave Perez a one-shot lead on the 18th tee. Despite appearing to need only to make par to seal his first victory, Perez kept the pedal to the metal, pounded his driver, and wound up out of bounds again. Perez could not make eagle with his second ball, which he needed to tie after Gogel made birdie at No. 18, an exclamation point to a well deserved and overdue win.

Davis Love III proved that sometimes it is

Tiger Woods

collegiately at nearby San Jose State, played with Singh in the final round and got a firsthand look at the Fijian's wizardry. "The man snap-hooked his first three drives," said Oberholser, at the time ranked 188th in the world. "I stripe my first three and make pars while he makes birdies. It's hard to compete with that." The only player to shoot four rounds in the 60s, Singh became the third foreign-born player to win the tournament, along with Australians Bruce Crampton in 1965, and Brett Ogle in 1993.

Comedian George Lopez joined the party in 2004—in mariachi pants no less. After struggling with an opening round 70, Lopez tucked a voodoo gris-gris bag in his back pocket and rode the mojo to rounds of 61–64 with pro partner and fellow fashion plate Jesper Parnevik. Lopez not only made the cut in his first try, he and Parnevik tied for third.

The 2005 edition concluded on Sunday but was effectively over on Thursday when Phil Mickelson scorched Spyglass Hill with an otherworldly 62. Bettering the course record by two strokes was akin to lopping a half minute off the world record in the mile. The first wire-to-wire winner since the tournament expanded to 72 holes in 1958, Mickelson stretched his three-stroke first round lead to four strokes after Friday and seven after Saturday. Mike Weir tried to make things interesting—he was the only golfer among the leaders to shoot in the 60s on Sunday—but Mickelson's lead proved as insurmountable as it was impressive. The real drama came from the team competition, where Bill Murray and pro partner Scott Simpson, having made the cut for only the second time since joining forces in 1993, came up just short in their bid to write a real-life Cinderella story.

The third time was the charm for Arron Oberholser. After finishing T4 and then T6 the two previous years, Oberholser closed the deal in 2006. In doing so, he became the fifth player

indeed better to be lucky than good on his way to a second AT&T Pro-Am title in 1992. Having surrendered his third round lead early in his round on Sunday, Love clawed his way back with impressive birdies at Nos. 8, 9, and 10. Leading by one at the par-3 12th hole, Love plunked a photographer on the foot. The ball could have gone any which way, but it wound up on the green—four feet from the cup. Love made that birdie then added another at No. 18, which proved to be key after Tom Lehman missed a five-foot birdie to tie on the last hole.

Following a second place finish, a tie for tenth, and a tie for third in his first three events of the year, Vijay Singh made the 2004 AT&T Pebble Beach National Pro-Am the first of nine tournament victories in a magical season that saw Singh earn over $10 million in prize money and wrest the No. 1 world ranking from Tiger Woods. Arron Oberholser, who played

3M Celebrity Challenge

to make this event their first Tour victory, along with John Cook in 1981, Steve Jones in 1988, Brett Ogle in 1993, and Matt Gogel in 2002. The former San Jose State star also joined the likes of Johnny Miller, Tom Watson, Ken Venturi, George Archer, and Bob Rosburg on the list of tournament champions with local ties. As in 2004, Oberholser started the final round with a share of the lead. A birdie at No. 2 combined with Mike Weir's double-bogey gave Oberholser a three-stroke cushion, which stretched to five strokes by the fourth hole. That would be Oberholser's ultimate margin of victory, matching the largest in tournament history.

Phil Mickelson managed to right his foundering ship at the 2007 AT&T Pro-Am. Following his nightmare finish at the U.S. Open at Winged Foot, an underwhelming performance at the Ryder Cup, and a missed cut the week before, Mickelson went wire-to-wire again to jumpstart a season that would include wins at The Players and the Deutsche Bank championships. Mickelson and Kevin Sutherland started Sunday tied, but Sutherland's respectable 71 proved no match for Mickelson's torrid 66, the low round of the day. Mickelson's thirtieth career PGA Tour victory placed him in elite company with Jack Nicklaus and Johnny Miller as three-time champions, trailing only Sam Snead, who won four, and five-time champion Mark O'Meara.

In winning that year's Jack Lemmon Award, presented annually to the amateur who helps his pro the most strokes, Michael Watson added third-generation crystal to the family trophy case: His father, Tom, won pro titles in 1977 and 1978, and his grandfather, Ray, took team honors with pro partner Leonard Dodson back in 1941.

Las Vegas bookmakers could not have posted odds high enough on the unexpected 2008 trifecta of Phil Mickelson missing the cut, Vijay Singh losing in a playoff, and Steve Lowery hoisting the trophy. Lowery's record heading into the week was 0 for 199 dating back to the 2000 Southern Farm Bureau Classic, which he won while the top players were all at the Tour Championship. The double-whammy of third round double bogeys on the 10th and 12th holes at Poppy Hills had Lowery flirting with the cut, but the 47-year-old more than made up for it with birdies on five of the last six holes. Stuck in a pack of 17 players within four shots of the lead heading into Sunday, Lowery fired another five birdies on the front nine at Pebble Beach on his way to a 68 and the clubhouse lead. Singh birdied the 18th to force the playoff but was unable to repeat the feat to extend the match. Lowery's birdie on the first extra hole was his third win on tour (his first coming at the 1994 Sprint International.) "This is absolutely my most meaningful win," said Lowery, for whom the two-year PGA Tour exemption was as sweet as the winner's check, which for the first time topped $1 million.

Rain by night giving way to clear skies by day made the golf courses ripe for scoring in 2009. Taking advantage of the soft conditions and the "lift, clean, and place" ruling, nearly half of the pros broke par on Thursday. Two-time U.S. Open winner Retief Goosen, playing in his first AT&T Pro-Am, jumped out to the second-round lead by two shots over 24-year-old Dustin Johnson, who played in the final pairing the year before but fell back and finished tied for seventh. Johnson had an inkling this might be a special week when his approach from 151 yards found the bottom of the cup for an eagle on no. 1 at Pebble Beach— Johnson's first hole of the tournament. Sleeping on a four-stroke Saturday night lead over Mike Weir, Johnson awoke Sunday to a wicked storm that blew the tarps off hospitality tents, knocked over a television tower, and uprooted a four-story pine tree along Pebble's third fairway.

"It probably would be a lot of ugly golf out there," said Weir, "but it would be kind of fun

Phil Mickelson

to see who could handle it." Monday morning the weather was better, relatively speaking, but ultimately unplayable, and for just the sixth time since the event expanded to four rounds in 1958, a 54-hole winner was declared. Johnson was eating breakfast when a fellow player called his cell phone with the good news. His reaction was one of mixed emotions: While he would have preferred to claim victory after a full four rounds, Johnson was plenty pleased to earn an inaugural invitation to the Masters and a return trip to the Monterey Peninsula as the defending champion of the AT&T Pebble Beach National Pro-Am.

2000

FEBRUARY 3–6

PEBBLE BEACH GOLF LINKS
POPPY HILLS GOLF COURSE
SPYGLASS HILL GOLF COURSE

PROFESSIONALS

Tiger Woods	1	68	73	68	64	273	$720,000
Matt Gogel	T2	69	68	67	71	275	
Vijay Singh	T2	66	67	72	70	275	

PRO-AM TEAMS

Skip Kendall	1	64	63	58	64	249
David Gill						
Tiger Woods	2	63	62	65	63	253
Jerry Chang						

Bernie Fuchs, ARTIST

2000

THE

AT&T PEBBLE BEACH

NATIONAL PRO-AM

pebble beach • poppy hills • spyglass hill

February 3-6, 2000 • Pebble Beach, California

2001

FEBRUARY 1–4

PEBBLE BEACH GOLF LINKS
POPPY HILLS GOLF COURSE
SPYGLASS HILL GOLF COURSE

PROFESSIONALS

Davis Love III	1	71	69	69	63	272	$720,000
Vijay Singh	2	66	68	70	69	273	
Phil Mickelson	T3	70	66	66	73	275	
Olin Browne	T3	68	69	65	73	275	

PRO-AM TEAMS

Tiger Woods	T1	59	67	64	64	254
Jerry Chang						
Phil Mickelson	T1	66	60	63	65	254
Kenny G						

THE
AT&T PEBBLE BEACH

pebble beach • poppy hills • spyglass hill

NATIONAL PRO-AM

February 1-4, 2001 • Pebble Beach, California

2002

JANUARY 31–FEBRUARY 3

PEBBLE BEACH GOLF LINKS
POPPY HILLS GOLF COURSE
SPYGLASS HILL GOLF COURSE

PROFESSIONALS

Matt Gogel	1	66	72	67	69	274	$720,000
Pat Perez	2	66	65	70	76	277	
Lee Janzen	T3	68	67	70	73	278	
Andrew Magee	T3	69	70	67	72	278	

PRO-AM TEAMS

Brian Claar Randall Mays	1	65	63	61	66	255
Craig Stadler Glenn Frey	2	60	66	66	64	256

THE

pebble beach • poppy hills • spyglass hill

AT&T PEBBLE BEACH

NATIONAL PRO-AM

Jan. 31 — Feb. 3, 2002 • Pebble Beach, California

2003

FEBRUARY 6–9

PEBBLE BEACH GOLF LINKS
POPPY HILLS GOLF COURSE
SPYGLASS HILL GOLF COURSE

PROFESSIONALS

Davis Love III	1	72	67	67	68	274	$900,000
Tom Lehman	2	68	70	70	67	275	
Mike Weir	T3	67	74	67	68	276	
Tim Herron	T3	69	69	72	66	276	

PRO-AM TEAMS

Brad Faxon	T1	66	63	64	64	257
Thomas Ryan						
Phil Tataurangi	T1	64	66	63	64	257
Craig Heatley						

THE

pebble beach • poppy hills • spyglass hill

AT&T PEBBLE BEACH

NATIONAL PRO-AM

FEBRUARY 3 – 9, 2003 • PEBBLE BEACH, CALIFORNIA

2004

FEBRUARY 5–8

PEBBLE BEACH GOLF LINKS
POPPY HILLS GOLF COURSE
SPYGLASS HILL GOLF COURSE

PROFESSIONALS

Vijay Singh	1	67	68	68	69	272	$954,000
Jeff Maggert	2	71	68	67	69	275	
Phil Mickelson	3	68	68	71	69	276	

PRO-AM TEAMS

Jerry Kelly	1	65	64	61	64	254
Robert Halmi Jr.						
Vijay Singh	2	66	62	62	66	256
Ted Forstmann						

THE
AT&T PEBBLE BEACH
NATIONAL PRO-AM

pebble beach • poppy hills • spyglass hill

Spyglass Hill #14

Poppy Hills #1

Pebble Beach Golf Links #7

FEBRUARY 2 – 8, 2004 • PEBBLE BEACH, CALIFORNIA

2005

FEBRUARY 10–13

PEBBLE BEACH GOLF LINKS
POPPY HILLS GOLF COURSE
SPYGLASS HILL GOLF COURSE

PROFESSIONALS

Phil Mickelson	1	62	67	67	73	269	$954,000
Mike Weir	2	66	67	73	67	273	
Greg Owen	3	67	69	67	72	275	

PRO-AM TEAMS

Joel Kribel Barry McCollam	1	63	63	63	64	253
Richard S. Johnson Bob Halloran	T2	64	63	64	66	257
Jay Delsing Doug Kintzinger	T2	58	65	66	68	257

Robb Havassy, ARTIST

THE AT&T PEBBLE BEACH
NATIONAL PRO-AM

pebble beach • poppy hills • spyglass hill

AT&T PEBBLE BEACH NATIONAL PRO-AM

FEBRUARY 7–13, 2005 • PEBBLE BEACH, CALIFORNIA

2006

FEBRUARY 9–12

PEBBLE BEACH GOLF LINKS
POPPY HILLS GOLF COURSE
SPYGLASS HILL GOLF COURSE

PROFESSIONALS

Arron Oberholser	1	65	68	66	72	271	$972,000
Rory Sabbatini	2	69	69	68	70	276	
Jonathan Byrd	T3	69	65	74	69	277	
Mike Weir	T3	63	67	69	78	277	

PRO-AM TEAMS

Arron Oberholser Michael McCallister	T1	59	65	63	68	255
Hunter Mahan Alan Heuer	T1	60	66	63	66	255

Bernie Fuchs ARTIST

THE
AT&T PEBBLE BEACH
NATIONAL PRO-AM

FEBRUARY 6–12, 2006 · PEBBLE BEACH, CALIFORNIA

PEBBLE BEACH · POPPY HILLS · SPYGLASS HILL

2007

FEBRUARY 8–11

PEBBLE BEACH GOLF LINKS
POPPY HILLS GOLF COURSE
SPYGLASS HILL GOLF COURSE

PROFESSIONALS

Phil Mickelson	1	65	67	70	66	268	$990,000
Kevin Sutherland	2	72	63	67	71	273	
John Mallinger	3	65	70	68	71	274	

PRO-AM TEAMS

Phil Mickelson Harry You	1	60	62	66	61	249
Tom Watson Michael Watson	2	65	62	66	60	253

The
AT&T PEBBLE BEACH
NATIONAL PRO-AM

FedExCup

FEBRUARY 5–11, 2007 • PEBBLE BEACH, CALIFORNIA
Pebble Beach • Poppy Hills • Spyglass Hill

at&t

2008

FEBRUARY 7–10

PEBBLE BEACH GOLF LINKS
POPPY HILLS GOLF COURSE
SPYGLASS HILL GOLF COURSE

PROFESSIONALS

Steve Lowery*	1	69	71	70	68	278	$1,080,000
Vijay Singh	2	70	70	67	71	278	
Dudley Hart	T3	69	70	68	72	279	
John Mallinger	T3	67	74	73	65	279	
Corey Pavin	T3	73	69	71	66	279	

*playoff

PRO-AM TEAMS

Fredrik Jacobson Bill Walters	1	65	62	62	61	250
D. A. Points Peter Watzka	2	64	69	66	61	260

The AT&T Pebble Beach National Pro-Am

Pebble Beach • Poppy Hills • Spyglass Hill
February 4-10, 2008

2009

PEBBLE BEACH GOLF LINKS
POPPY HILLS GOLF COURSE
SPYGLASS HILL GOLF COURSE

PROFESSIONALS

Dustin Johnson	1	65	69	67	201	$1,098,000
Mike Weir	2	67	69	69	205	
Retief Goosen	3	68	64	74	206	

PRO-AM TEAMS

| Dustin Johnson | T1 | 63 | 67 | 63 | 193 |
| Joe Rice | | | | | |

| Chris Stroud | T1 | 63 | 63 | 67 | 193 |
| Ron Christman | | | | | |

Scott Medlock, ARTIST

following page 2010 Suzanne Yost McCoy, ARTIST

The AT&T Pebble Beach National Pro-Am

Pebble Beach | Poppy Hills | Spyglass Hill | February 9-15, 2009

A Charitable Classic Since 1947

The AT&T Pebble Beach National Pro-Am

Pebble Beach Golf Links   Spyglass Hill Golf Course   Monterey Peninsula Country Club   February 8-14, 2010

AT&T PEBBLE BEACH NATIONAL PRO-AM

LEADERS	1 2 3 4 5 6 7 8 9 10 11 12 13 14 15 16 17 18	ROUND SCORES
2009 Dustin JOHNSON		1997 Mark O'MEARA
2008 Steve LOWERY		1996 El Niño
2007 Phil MICKELSON		1995 Peter JACOBSEN
2006 Arron OBERHOLSER		1994 Johnny MILLER
2005 Phil MICKELSON		1993 Brett OGLE
2004 Vijay SINGH		1992 Mark O'MEARA
2003 Davis LOVE III		1991 Paul AZINGER
2002 Matt GOGEL		1990 Mark O'MEARA
2001 Davis LOVE III		1989 Mark O'MEARA
2000 Tiger WOODS		1988 Steve JONES
1999 Payne STEWART		1987 Johnny MILLER
1998 Phil MICKELSON		1986 Fuzzy ZOELLER

Suzanne Yost McCourt

A Charitable Classic
Since 1947

AT&T PEBBLE BEACH NATIONAL PRO-AM

at&t

PGA TOUR   FedEx Cup